Jung's Function-Attitudes Explained

Jung's Function-Attitudes Explained

Henry L. Thompson, Ph.D.

Foreword By
Margaret T. Hartzler, Ph.D.

Wormhole Publishing
Watkinsville, Georgia

General Editor: *D. Grenae Thompson*
Editorial Assistants: *L. Michele Thompson, Gerald W. Bruce & Norma Pettigrew*
Interior Graphics: *Merry G. Maxey*
Cover Design: *High Performing Systems, Inc.*
Printing and Binding: *Athens Printing Company*

Permissions
A Cognitive Perspective on Jungian Typology by James Newman. Copyright ©1990 by James Newman. Excerpts reprinted with permission of James Newman.

"Beebe's Model" graphics, copyright ©1990 by John Beebe, are reprinted with permission of John Beebe.

The quotation on page 96 modified and reproduced by special permission of the Publisher, Consulting Psychologists Press, Inc., Palo Alto, CA 94303, from *Katharine and Isabel: Mother's Light, Daughter's Journey* by Frances Wright Saunders. Copyright 1991 by Consulting Psychologists Press, Inc. All rights reserved. Further reproduction is prohibited without the Publisher's written consent.

Jung's Typology by M-L Von Franz and J. Hillman. Copyright ©1971 by Spring Publications, Inc. Excerpts, cited passim, are reprinted with permission of Spring Publications, Inc.

"Marshall's Model of Consciousness" graphic, copyright ©1991 by Allen Marshall, is reprinted with permission of Allen Marshall.

Myers-Briggs Type Indicator® and MBTI® are registered trademarks of Consulting Psychologists Press, Inc.

Personality Types: Jung's Model of Typology by Daryl Sharp. Copyright ©1987 by Daryl Sharp. Excerpts reprinted with permission of Daryl Sharp.

Psychological Types, a revision by R. F. C. Hull of the translation by H. G. Baynes. Copyright ©1976 by Princeton University Press. Excerpts, cited passim, are reprinted with permission of Princeton University Press.

Library of Congress Cataloging-in-Publication Data

Thompson, Henry L., 1947–
    Jung's Function-Attitudes Explained / Henry L. Thompson
        p.   cm.
    Includes bibliographical references and index.
    ISBN: 1-887278-01-X
    1. Typology (Psychology)   2. Myers-Briggs Type Indicator.
    3. Jung, C. G. (Carl Gustav), 1875-1961.   I. Title.
                                    96-61225
                                    CIP
Printed in the United States of America   ISBN: 1-887278-01-X

10 9 8 7 6 5 4 3 2 1

To my parents, Henry and Christine

Contents

Foreword

Many practitioners of Type have lost the essence of the Jungian Types because they only deal with the four functions: Sensing, iNtuiting, Feeling and Thinking. Carl Jung defined his Types according to the dominant function and whether it was used in an extraverted or introverted manner. When you look at Type from a function-attitude perspective, there are not four functions, but eight: the four perceiving function-attitudes—introverted Sensing, extraverted Sensing, introverted iNtuiting, extraverted iNtuiting; and the four judging function-attitudes—introverted Thinking, extraverted Thinking, introverted Feeling and extraverted Feeling.

This is the first book to focus exclusively on the eight function-attitudes as they manifest themselves in the dominant and inferior positions and, as such, pulls together disparate literature into an invaluable resource. Dr. Thompson transcends the usual presentation of function-attitudes by presenting unique graphic representations, image labels, memory functions and new ways of looking at these eight function-attitudes that I think the reader will find useful in grasping underlying concepts that are sometimes very elusive. Whereas Isabel Myers went to great lengths to present Type descriptions in positive terms, Dr. Thompson presents the "positive" and the "negative" in his interpretive descriptions of the function-attitude Types.

I believe that within the next few years, people who use the MBTI and Type theory will be introducing their clients to the eight function-attitudes during initial feedback sessions. Therefore, it is crucial that we continue to refine and expand our understanding of what the eight Jungian function-attitudes bring to the sixteen Types as defined by Isabel Myers and Katharine Briggs.

Margaret T. Hartzler, Ph.D.

Margaret T. Hartzler, Ph.D., is an MBTI practitioner, author of *Making Type Work For You: A Resource Book* and numerous articles, an MBTI qualifying program trainer and principal in Type Resources, Inc.

Preface

Over the years I have spent a great deal of time researching and ferreting out pieces of information about Jung's function-attitudes from Jung's writings, the work of other prominent Jungians, and supporters of Isabel B. Myers and the Myers-Briggs Type Indicator (MBTI). This pursuit of information about the function-attitudes stems from the fact that to understand Jung's system of psychological Type, one must understand the dynamics of the function-attitudes and their interactions.

Although Jung concentrated his thoughts about the function-attitudes in his book *Psychological Types*, he scattered additional thoughts and concepts about them through various other writings. His followers, such as C. A. Meier, Marie-Louise von Franz and James Hillman, have also presented short discussions of the function-attitudes from their own perspectives. This leaves students of psychological Type to search out and decipher various writings about the function-attitudes on their own. This book provides a consolidated source for learning about the basics of the function-attitudes, along with some new perspectives.

The book is intended for the use of trainers and practitioners who already have a basic understanding of Jung's and Myers' concepts of psychological Type. The growing use of the MBTI—Consulting Psychologists Press, Inc., reports one million or more administrations a year—dictates a need for a definitive resource on the function-attitudes for the practitioner.

Because this is written as a reference work, I have tried to not stray too far from Jungian theory and have quoted heavily from Jung's work. I have also found that MBTI practitioners in particular do not always like Jung's descriptions of the Types or his explanations of the cognitive processes at work. Thus, some readers might find certain passages in this book hard to accept, especially those that describe characteristics of the reader's Type preference that the reader does not like. Isabel Myers expended a lot of effort to make the Myers-Briggs Type descriptions positive and, therefore, acceptable to the reader. Jung tended to be more blunt in his descriptions. Perhaps this is an example of a stylistic difference between a Feeler (Myers) and a Thinker (Jung).

Like other practitioners using the MBTI, I have found that 15-25% of people have difficulty validating one or more of the functions as they are normally presented in basic MBTI classes. One of the difficulties of validating a function is that the basic presentations typically give only generic function descriptions, i.e., a description of a "pure" function such as Sensing. Someone with a preference for introverted Sensing can identify with the introverted

Sensing part of the generic description of Sensing, but not necessarily with the extraverted part. This has led Margaret Hartzler and her colleagues to include the function-attitudes descriptions in their basic MBTI classes.

Chapter 1 provides an overview of Jung's typology and the Myers and Briggs extension of it as a review and lead-in to a detailed discussion of attitudes, functions and function-attitudes. Although advanced practitioners will not find anything earth-shattering in this chapter, new practitioners will find that it helps clarify the relationship of Jungian and Myers-Briggs concepts and the Myers-Briggs theory in particular. It is also a good beginning place for even the advanced practitioner.

In Chapter 2 the reader is introduced to Jung's original concept of psychic energy flow, which creates what he referred to as "attitudes." The descriptions of his attitude Types and the origin of Jung's interest in psychological Type are also presented. The attitude Type was his first theory of psychological Type—the primordial soup of his typology theory—and his focus for the first ten years of his work on typology.

Chapter 3 provides the next step in the evolution of Jung's typology—the introduction of the perceiving and judging processes and the four functions: Sensing, iNtuiting, Thinking and Feeling. Each of these functions is examined in its relationship to the other functions and for its impact on the cognitive and behavioral aspects of personality. To assist the reader in making contrasts of the opposite poles of the perceiving and judging processes, contrast Tables are presented as summaries along with graphics that summarize each function.

The end of this chapter presents one of Jung's more obscure concepts relating to the functions—operating modes. The four types of operating modes—active and passive, abstract and concrete—are described and summarized.

Chapter 4 presents the third major developmental step in Jung's typology, the combining of functions and attitudes to create his eight classic function-attitudes: extraverted Sensing, introverted Sensing, extraverted iNtuiting, introverted iNtuiting, extraverted Thinking, introverted Thinking, extraverted Feeling and introverted Feeling. This chapter focuses on the perceiving function-attitudes (extraverted Sensing, introverted Sensing, extraverted iNtuiting, introverted iNtuiting) and establishes a unique presentation format. The function-attitudes are given "image labels" (a descriptive word, e.g., "sensuosity" for extraverted Sensing) to help the reader create an image of the function-attitude process. Additionally, graphics are presented as a summary of the characteristics of each of the perceiving function-attitudes.

Chapter 5 follows the same format as Chapter 4 and focuses on the judging function-attitudes (extraverted Thinking, introverted Thinking, extraverted Feeling and introverted Feeling).

Chapter 6 presents an overview of Type development, including the models of John Beebe, Allen Marshall and Angelo Spoto. Briefly, it also looks at Type using Allen Marshall's model of consciousness and my own systems model of psychological Type. This chapter points out the flaws in using a linear approach to the study of typology and points the way to the future—the use of a systems approach.

The exercises in the Appendix allow a person to experience the impact of the function-attitudes in a controlled environment. These are powerful exercises that can be used with participants in counseling and training sessions to make the function-attitudes processes more salient.

Feedback from readers of the original manuscript confirmed my expectation of the need for a book such as this one. As an introverted iNtuiting Type, I see this book as a thought-in-process, not a final answer or even a stepping stone toward the next level of understanding of psychological Type. It is an interim "fix," a bandage on a bleeding artery that will have to suffice until systems theories move us into a new paradigm that allows us to gain some understanding of cosmic relationships.

Acknowledgments

The author wishes to express his gratitude to the following people:

Grenae Thompson, for her continuous support and encouragement over the past 25 years that enabled me to position myself to write this book. Without her this book would not exist. She provided personal support and insight that only an iNtuiting Feeling Type could have provided during the preparation of the manuscript. Her unique creative ability, editorial and writing skills, and feedback were invaluable in shaping my thoughts and, ultimately, this project. Nowhere could I have found a more perfect mate.

My children, Michele, Stephen and Jennifer, for providing numerous Type examples as they were growing up.

My brother, CW4 Larry K. (Butch) Thompson, for providing key insights into the dynamics of the introverted Sensing Type.

Merry G. Maxey, for her graphics skills, creativity, relentless pursuit to obtain factual graphics and gracious attitude during the many revisions.

Donna Hammond, for typing manuscripts, providing introverted Sensing insights and, above all, demonstrating for the rest of us how to keep a positive attitude during extreme adversity.

A SPECIAL THANKS to Margaret T. Hartzler, Allen Marshall, Angelo Spoto, Dan R. Bruffey, Tricia A. Evert, Will Rives and John Beebe for their time, effort and valuable comments while reviewing the book manuscript.

My thanks also to Terri Dorsey, Joe Brand, Karen Marshall, Mary Bales, Cindy Doniel, Karen Winter, Karen Ridout and Tracey Daley for reading and commenting on particular sections of the manuscript; and to Type practitioners, workshop and seminar participants, with whom I have interacted over the last eighteen years in testing the various aspects of the function-attitudes concepts. Their knowledge, insights and thoughts shared during these interactions helped make this a viable explanation of Jung's function-attitude Types.

Typology

It is not the purpose of a psychological typology to classify human beings into categories; this in itself would be pretty pointless. Its purpose is to provide a critical psychology which will make a methodological investigation and presentation of the empirical material possible. (Jung, 1976a, p. 554)

Historically, numerous attempts have been made to categorize human behavior into elaborate typology systems. Figure 1 shows an abbreviated flow of various typologies beginning almost twenty-five hundred years ago with Hippocrates (circa 450 B.C.). The diagram separates the development of typologies into two relatively distinct schools, *temperament* and *psychological Type*[1], both of which attempt to make the same basic predictions about the "hows" and "whys" of human behavior. Temperament follows a basic quadratic model. The most prominent of the temperament typologies today is David Keirsey's (1978) model with four classifications: *Guardian, Artisan, Idealist* and *Rationalist*.

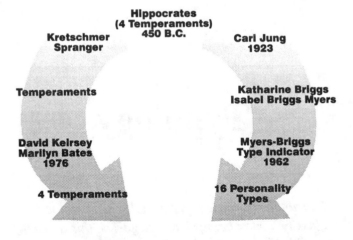

Figure 1
Historical Perspective

Psychological Type has evolved primarily from the work of C. G. Jung and takes a more expanded approach—sixteen

---

[1] The word "type" will be capitalized whenever it refers to psychological Type.

Types vs. four temperaments. One of the most widely used forms of psychological Type is the variation of Jung's model developed by Isabel B. Myers and Katharine C. Briggs and measured by the Myers-Briggs Type Indicator[2]. As psychological Type continues its rapid growth in popularity, both in the United States and globally, the need for more usable, reader-friendly resources on particular aspects of C. G. Jung's original theory becomes paramount.

Over the past ten years I have observed an increasing hunger on the part of the psychological Type community (especially those practitioners using the Myers-Briggs Type Indicator) for "understandable" information on the deeper meaning of the more obscure, although often-mentioned, components of Jung's theory. The purpose of this book is to pull together key information and concepts about Jung's *function-attitude Types* from disparate sources—relying very heavily on Jung's writings—and to provide a discussion of them in a single, practical, easy-to-understand source.

Although the assumption is made that the reader has at least an introductory knowledge of Jung's theory of psychological Types, the Myers-Briggs' variation of Jung's work and the Myers-Briggs Type Indicator (MBTI), a brief overview of each will be presented as a starting point. For advanced practitioners who may wish to skip ahead, these chapters are presented in stand-alone fashion. The references listed at the end of this book contain much more information than this short presentation allows.

The format of the book is shown in Figure 2, proceeding from a general overview that slowly begins to intertwine Jungian views with those of the Myers-Briggs community to create a unique perspective on the function-attitude Types.

---

[2] Myers-Briggs Type Indicator® and MBTI® are registered trademarks of Consulting Psychologists Press, Inc.

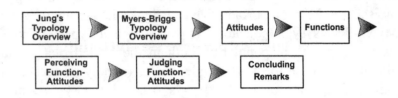

Figure 2
Discussion Flow

Jung's Typology Overview

Jung's typology is typically over-simplified as a two-dimensional model with the four *functions* of Sensing and iNtuiting[3] as polar opposites on one dimension and Thinking and Feeling at opposite poles on the other (see Figure 3). Although this model does allow for the graphic depiction of the polar "opposites" relationship of the perceiving functions (Sensing and iNtuiting) and the judging functions (Thinking and Feeling), it does little to portray the magnitude of complexity in Jung's theory. This overview will also present an oversimplification of Jung's typology. More in-depth insight about specific relevant concepts will be provided in later chapters.

---

[3] I have long agreed with Dr. Margaret Hartzler that the function "names" should be parallel and will follow her recommendation of using "iNtuiting" in place of intuitive. The "N" in iNtuiting will be capitalized rather than the "I," because the I is reserved for the introverted attitude in the MBTI Type code.

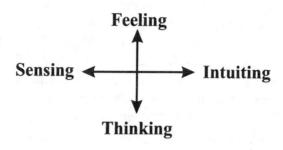

Figure 3
The Functional Polarities

Jung's typology is a *dynamic, systemic* approach to a *psychology of consciousness* that deals with the "problem of opposites" (Spoto, 1995). His typology centers around the individual's *psyche*, defined by Jung to mean all *cognitive* processes, both conscious and unconscious. It manifests in the form of *psychic energy*[4] (*libido*) that is capable of morphing into many different forms. Initially, Jung visualized psychic energy as flowing out of the psyche to the outer world of objects, people and things; or inward to the subjective world of ideas, thoughts and feelings. He termed this energy flow *attitude*. Attitude was directed (flowed) to the outer world or the inner world. Jung discovered that the direction of flow of psychic energy could be identified in a particular person by observing that person's behavior. Individuals whose energy habitually flowed to the outside were of the *extraverted attitude* and classified as *extraverted Types*. If energy habitually flowed to the inside, they were of the *introverted attitude* and classified as *introverted Types*.

---

[4] The proposition that libido could have many forms, not just sexual, was one of the major disputes between Jung and Freud that led to the separation of the Vienna and Zürich schools (Spoto, 1995).

After a number of years of additional study and observation, Jung expanded his typology by adding four functions: *Sensing*, *iNtuiting*, *Thinking* and *Feeling*. These functions provided additional means for the psyche to adapt to the outer and inner worlds. Like the attitudes, functions are polar opposites. That is, extraversion and introversion are on opposite poles from each other, Sensing and iNtuiting are on opposite poles, and so are Thinking and Feeling. This polar concept has far-reaching implications for the dynamics of the different components of Jungian typology. As opposites, either extraversion or introversion controls the flow of psychic energy at a particular time. Both cannot be in control at the same instant. For example, you cannot be very talkative (extraverted) and very quiet (introverted) at the same instant. The same applies to the functions. Only one of each dipole can be in consciousness at a time, and more specifically, only one of the four functions can be in *control* of consciousness at any particular instant.

It is important to note that the dipolar relationship only implies singularity of use, not exclusivity. When teaching, I often use two physical metaphors to make this point. The first is to have participants cross their arms. Then on command, quickly reverse them (cross them the opposite way). What they will notice about this exercise, and the most obvious and important point, is that they were able to reverse them—some might have to keep trying, but they will eventually accomplish it! They notice that it took more time to reverse their arms, they had to think more, it might have been uncomfortable and, in general, they were less proficient at the task in the reversed mode. Similarly, people have a preference between Sensing and iNtuiting. If their preference is Sensing, it is like the way they crossed their arms the first time—fast, easy and comfortable. When they use iNtuiting, it is like reversing the arms; it just doesn't feel as natural.

A second metaphor is to have participants write their names on a piece of paper. Then have them write them again, except this time using their non-preferred hand. They will notice a significant difference in penmanship. They get more practice (and develop more skill) with their preferred writing hand. When they are writing with one hand, the other is not being used; consequently, it does not become as skilled. In both metaphors, however, they were able to use the other, non-preferred dipole—just not as proficiently.

Figure 3 shows the basic polar relationship Jung initially established between the functions. Sensing and iNtuiting are described as *perceiving* functions because they are the only functions capable of perceiving stimuli. Thinking and Feeling are *judging* functions because they judge all perceptions. Like the attitudes, if a person shows a preference for the habitual use of one of the functions over the others, he or she is said to have *differentiated* that function above the others and is identified by that function, e.g., a Thinking Type. In the writing metaphor above, if you have differentiated your writing skills with your right hand you are typically called right-handed.

Jung's (1976a) typology is a *dynamic* system. This implies an interaction among the components of the system. For example, a person might have a habitual attitude, such as extraversion, and a habitual function, such as Thinking, which interact in a way that results in an extraverted Thinking Type. In fact, Jung found that the attitudes and functions combined to form eight function-attitude Types; extraverted Sensing; extraverted iNtuiting; extraverted Thinking; extraverted Feeling; introverted Sensing; introverted iNtuiting; introverted Thinking; and introverted Feeling. Jung states that

> *Closer investigation shows with great regularity that, besides the most differentiated function, another, less differentiated function of secondary importance is invariably present in consciousness and exerts a co-determining influence.* (p. 405)

With this revelation, Jung significantly expanded the scope and complexity of his typology. A primary and a secondary function can combine to form what are commonly known in MBTI terminology (Myers, 1980) as *functional* pairs. The polarity constraint on the functions restricts certain combinations of functions. For example, Sensing and iNtuiting cannot combine[5] and neither can Thinking and Feeling because they are dipoles. Thus, there are four basic combinations: Sensing Thinking; Sensing Feeling; iNtuiting Thinking; iNtuiting Feeling. Each function also has an associated attitude. Although Jung stated that these pairings take place, he did not give behavioral descriptions of the result of each pairing.

Another of Jung's discoveries was that if the primary (most differentiated) function had an extraverted attitude, e.g., extraverted Sensing, then the secondary function had the opposite attitude, e.g. introverted Thinking, giving a function-attitude pair of extraverted Sensing/introverted Thinking. Specific, identifiable behavior results from not only each pairing, but also from the most differentiated function. Table 1 shows the combinations of the function-attitudes representing the sixteen psychological Types.

Table 1 is often an "aha!" experience for Myers-Briggs Type practitioners because the psychological Type literature gives Jung credit for defining only eight psychological Types (function-attitude Types) while Myers and Briggs are credited with taking his eight Types and expanding them to sixteen Types. Although Jung indirectly defined the sixteen Types above, he did not articulate behavioral descriptions beyond the eight function-attitude Types.

---

[5] Jung stated that functions always formed perceiving-judging pairs. Chapter 6 presents alternative hypotheses.

Extraverted Function Types		Introverted Function Types	
Extraverted Sensing/ Introverted Thinking	Extraverted Sensing/ Introverted Feeling	Introverted Sensing/ Extraverted Thinking	Introverted Sensing/ Extraverted Feeling
Extraverted iNtuiting/ Introverted Thinking	Extraverted iNtuiting/ Introverted Feeling	Introverted iNtuiting/ Extraverted Thinking	Introverted iNtuiting/ Extraverted Feeling
Extraverted Thinking/ Introverted Sensing	Extraverted Thinking/ Introverted iNtuiting	Introverted Thinking/ Extraverted Sensing	Introverted Thinking/ Extraverted iNtuiting
Extraverted Feeling/ Introverted Sensing	Extraverted Feeling/ Introverted iNtuiting	Introverted Feeling/ Extraverted Sensing	Introverted Feeling/ Extraverted iNtuiting

Note: The primary function-attitude is listed first in each pair.

Table 1
Primary-Secondary Combinations

Another key component of Jung's typology is his concept of the *inferior* function. When a function becomes differentiated to the degree that it becomes *superior* to the others (becomes the primary function), it does so at the expense of its polar opposite. For example, when Sensing becomes differentiated to the degree that it becomes superior to the other functions, iNtuiting becomes the least differentiated of all or, in Jung's terms, the inferior function. Jung's (1976a) rationale is that when Sensing is in use, iNtuiting cannot be used because it is diametrically opposed to Sensing. The more Sensing is used (and developed), the less iNtuiting is developed, thus making iNtuiting inferior.

The significance of the inferior function is twofold. The first is that being inferior, this function tends to manifest in a more primitive and archaic form when it enters consciousness. Thus, we tend not to be very proficient at using it. In the handwriting metaphor above, using your inferior function would be like writing your name using the toes on your left foot to hold the pencil. The terminology *in the grip* is frequently used to describe the behavior of someone whose consciousness has been temporarily taken over by the inferior function.

The second significance of the inferior function is that it supports the implication of a sequence of use and development. Jung defined the primary (superior) function as the most differentiated, the secondary function as the next most differentiated and the inferior as the least differentiated. This leaves one other function, the opposite of the secondary. This function logically falls between the secondary and the inferior, making it the tertiary function. Now all four functions have been sequenced based on differentiation and developmental sequence. For example, if the primary is Sensing and the secondary Feeling, then the resulting sequence would be as follows (Table 2).

Primary	Secondary	Tertiary	Inferior
Sensing	Feeling	Thinking	iNtuiting

Table 2
Function Sequence

The above is intended only as a superficial, encapsulated view of *part* of Jung's typology. More information and explanation will follow as the discussion focuses on the specific function-attitudes. Students of Jung soon discover that just beneath the surface of Jung's typology in *Psychological Types* (1976a) lies an exceedingly complex theory. It is so complex that many readers do not finish the book, much less understand what they have read. Fortunately, Isabel Myers and Katharine Briggs did understand it, and working together, found a way to expand and articulate it in a comprehensible manner.

Myers-Briggs Typology Overview

One of the most popular instruments for assessing psychological Type today is the Myers-Briggs Type Indicator, with over a million assessments a year being reported. The MBTI is an adaptation of Jung's typology formatted for ease of understanding by the general population. The work was originated by Katharine Cooke Briggs when she set out to develop her own typology based on patterns she found while reading biographies. She identified and labeled four "Types": *meditative*, *spontaneous*, *executive* and *sociable*. Later when she discovered Jung's book *Psychological Types*, she told her daughter, Isabel, that she had found the typology for which she had been searching. This mother-daughter team spent the next twenty years studying Jung's work and watching "Types" together.

Isabel Briggs Myers[6] made the development of an understandable and useful typology her life's quest. She developed the "Indicator" to allow for the assessment of Type and continued to develop and refine the MBTI, databases, Type descriptions and their uses until her death in 1980. Her book *Gifts Differing* (1980) was published shortly after her death and provides the best overview of her typology available. It is required reading for any student of typology.

Myers and Briggs developed a shorthand for depicting a Type code. They began by assigning letters to replace the attitude and function names, e.g., "E" for extravert, "I" for introvert, "S" for Sensing, "N" for iNtuiting, "T" for Thinking and "F" for Feeling. This enabled them to represent the functional pairs by using only two letters, always in the perceiving-judging sequence, such as ST, SF, NT and NF. To identify the attitude of the

---

[6] Isabel Briggs Myers (INFP) was born on October 18, 1897, married Clarence ("Chief") G. Myers in 1918, and died of cancer in 1980. She was truly a remarkable woman and a pioneer in the areas of typology and improving relationships through the understanding of differences.

dominant[7] function, they began the Type code with its attitude (E or I)—*noted first because Jung considered it so important.* For example, if an individual has a functional pair of extraverted Sensing/introverted Feeling and Sensing is the dominant function, the first three letters of the Type code would be ESF because Sensing is extraverted in this example. If Feeling is the dominant function in this example, then the code is ISF because Feeling is introverted. *The first letter in the Type code identifies the attitude of the dominant function and the direction of flow of psychic energy.*

Myers and Briggs struggled with how the individual Type adapted to the outer world. The result of their study was the addition of the bipolar *orientation* dimension to Jung's attitude, perceiving and judging model. The poles of the orientation dipole were described as judging (J) and perceiving (P). *The assignment of the orientation identifier (J or P) is determined by the function with the extraverted attitude in the functional pair.* If the individual's perceiving function (S or N) is extraverted, then the perceiving orientation identifier (P) is assigned to the end of the Type code. If the judging function (T or F) has the extraverted attitude, the judging orientation identifier (J) is added. For example, if a person's Type is extraverted Sensing/introverted Thinking (ST), then the perceiving (P) identifier is assigned, i.e., STP. If the functional pair is introverted Sensing/extraverted Thinking (ST), the identifier is J, i.e., STJ. The orientation dimension identifies which function in the functional pair is used in an extraverted mode. *The last letter in the Type code identifies the extraverted function.*

---

[7] In the development of their model, Myers and Briggs modified some of Jung's terminology to make it more meaningful to the average person. Two examples are replacing "primary" function with "dominant" function and "secondary" with "auxiliary."

When the attitude, functions and orientation are combined, they form the complete four-letter Type code—the "letters" for which the MBTI is famous. For example, an extraverted iNtuiting/introverted Feeling Type with iNtuiting as the dominant function would be assigned the Type code ENFP. The "P" identifies the perceptive function, iNtuiting, as the extraverted function and the "E" indicates the extraverted function, iNtuiting, is also the dominant function. In an ISTJ, the "J" identifies the judging function, Thinking, as the extraverted function and the "I" indicates that the introverted function, Sensing, is the dominant function. For extraverted Types the extraverted function is dominant, for introverted Types the extraverted function is not the dominant. Table 3 shows the code components of two Type examples with the dominant function bolded.

Attitude of Dominant Function	Perceiving Function	Judging Function	Identifier of Extraverted Function
E	**N**	F	P
I	**S**	T	J

Table 3
Type Code

New students of MBTI often struggle with how to look at a Type code and easily identify which function is dominant. Isabel B. Myers (1979) wrote a rhyme to resolve the problem of which function is dominant.

> *An extravert who has forgotten his*
> *can ask JP which one it is.*
> *But when an introvert's forgot,*
> *JP tells him which one it's not!*

The Type code, as shown above, made a significant contribution to the understandability of Jung's theory for the layperson. The visual representation of a Type made it much easier to remember and recognize differences. The Type code also allowed for the creation of the very popular MBTI Type preferences model, typically depicted as sixteen four-letter "Types" and often arranged in a "Type table" as shown in Table 4.

ISTJ	ISFJ	INFJ	INTJ
ISTP	ISFP	INFP	INTP
ESTP	ESFP	ENFP	ENTP
ESTJ	ESFJ	ENFJ	ENTJ

Table 4
Myers-Briggs Type Table

Type *preference* connotes special meaning about a person's Type and interaction of Type variables far beyond the four letters in the Type code. In a sense, the Type preference is like a strand of *personality DNA*. The preferences and degree of differentiation form a blueprint for the dynamics of an individual's personality.

This overview of Jung's typology and the Myers-Briggs extension and simplification provide the foundation for a more extensive discussion of the function-attitudes. Before discussing the function-attitudes in detail, a review of the attitudes (Chapter 2) and functions (Chapter 3) will be presented to assist in clarifying the effects of the interaction of attitudes and functions.

Attitude Types

I shall attempt a general description of the psychology of the types, starting with the two basic types I have termed introverted and extraverted. This will be followed by a description of those more special types whose peculiarities are due to the fact that the individual adapts and orients himself chiefly by means of his most differentiated function. The former I would call attitude-types, distinguished by the direction of their interest, or of the movement of libido; the latter I would call function-types. (Jung, 1976a, p. 330)

Jung's initial inquiries into psychological Type revolved around the question of the *focus* of one's psychic energy. Was it on the *object*[8] (the external world) as with Sigmund Freud, or was it on the *subject* (the internal world) as in the case of Alfred Adler[9]? Jung felt that both were necessary, although they could be seen differentiated to varying degrees in people. From his association with both Freud and Adler, it was obvious that Freud's focus was on the object (the external world) and Adler's focus was on the subject (the internal world).

> *The Freudian theory is attractively simple, so much so that it almost pains one if anybody drives in the wedge of a contrary assertion. But the same is true of Adler's theory. It too is of illuminating simplicity and explains as much as the Freudian theory. . . . But how comes it that each investigator sees only one valid view? . . . Both are obviously working with the same material: but because of personal peculiarities they each see things from a different angle.* (Jung, 1976b, para 56f)

Jung (1976b) labels the objective-versus-subjective approaches of Freud and Adler as the same problem—

---

[8] When Jung refers to the **object** he is referring to things located outside of the psyche, often defined as "reality" or "physical stimuli" such as a flower, noise, people, etc. The internal, physiological functions of the body are also considered part of the object. The object is the world external to the psyche. The **subject** refers to the internal world—that which occurs inside the psyche, e.g., a hunch, memory, idea, etc.

[9] Jung met Freud for the first time in 1907 and teamed up with him and his star student Adler. The alliance lasted for five years with Adler splitting from Freud first, followed soon by Jung (Spoto, 1995).

complementary *attitude-Types* or *polarities* that exist in all people, even infants. Thus, Jung thought attitudes to be of a biological origin. His quest to understand the difference between Freud and Adler launched his original Type theory that consisted of categorizing behavior into the attitude Types of *extraversion* (externally focused) or *introversion* (internally focused).

Extraversion

Those who show a preference for extraversion (E) focus on (place into consciousness) the outer world of people, places and things, referred to as the "object" by Jung.

> *Now, when orientation by the object predominates in such a way that decisions and actions are determined not by subjective views but by objective conditions, we speak of an extraverted attitude. When this is habitual, we speak of an extraverted type. If a man thinks, feels, acts and actually lives in a way that is* directly *correlated with the objective conditions and their demands, he is extraverted.* (Jung, 1976a, p. 333)

Thus, extraverts are externally focused and driven. The outer world garners all their attention and psychic energy, with little left over for internal, subjective matters. Extraverts tend to be energized by being around others and become bored or drained if they spend too much time alone. They usually have good verbal skills and prefer to think aloud and discuss their thoughts with others, resulting in the occasional "foot (or feet)-in-the-mouth" syndrome. At gatherings they tend to speak out easily and are not hesitant to meet new people. The old saying "what you see is what you get" holds true for most extraverts, at least in terms of their psychological Type.

Introversion

Introverts (I), on the other hand, have their energy consumed by the inner world of ideas, thoughts and feelings, the "subjective" in Jung's terminology. The outer world has little meaning and becomes a significant energy drain if the person has to spend very much time in it.

> *Although the introverted consciousness is naturally aware of external conditions, it selects the subjective determinants as the decisive ones. It is therefore oriented by the factor in perception and cognition which responds to the sense stimulus in accordance with the individual's subjective disposition.* (Jung, 1976a, pp. 373-374)

Consequently, introverts value their time alone. When working on a problem, they often prefer to work it out alone using their introspective strengths. Since their focus is on the subjective, they tend to be reserved in meetings, hesitate to make new acquaintances and, in general, might seem difficult to get to know. They often suffer from the "why-didn't-I-say-that" syndrome—hesitating to answer until an extravert has answered, the topic has changed or the opportunity has passed. I like to compare introverts to pipe smokers. If you ask a question of a pipe smoker who has just lit his pipe, he will take a couple of puffs from his pipe, dump out the tobacco, remove a tool kit from his pocket, clean out the insides of his pipe, change the "carburetor," refill the pipe, light it, take a couple of puffs, look you in the eye and reply, "I don't know." Introverts like to take time to reflect before answering. Unlike the extravert, the introvert tends to be full of surprises—what you see is not necessarily what you get!

Attitude Compensation

Jung's *law of compensation*[10] is at work with the attitude polarity in that while the extravert's conscious[11] energy flow is outward toward the object, there is a compensating response of introversion into the unconscious to balance the process. If this process becomes unbalanced, neuroses and physical symptoms may develop.

> *The extraverted type is constantly tempted to expend himself for the apparent benefit of the object, to assimilate subject to object. I have discussed in some detail the harmful consequences of exaggeration of the extraverted attitude.* (Jung, 1976a, p. 337)

Singer (1994) states, *"People who are extraverted in the extreme may behave in a manic or hysterical manner, or they may suffer from psychosomatic illnesses, all in a pathological effort to control the environment and the people in it"* (p. 328). Extreme extraverts might be so talkative and driven by the external environment that people (even other extraverts) avoid them because they find their behavior obnoxious.

---

[10] Jung (1976a) defines compensation as a normally unconscious self-regulation of the psychic apparatus. *"I regard the activity of the* unconscious (q.v.) *as a balancing of the one-sidedness of the general* attitude (q.v.) *produced by the function of* consciousness (q.v.)*"* (p. 419).

[11] Jung (1976a) defines consciousness as *"the relation of psychic contents to the ego (q.v.), in so far as the relation is perceived by the ego. Relations to the ego that are not perceived as such are* unconscious (q.v.)*. Consciousness is the function or activity which maintains the relation of psychic contents to the ego"* (pp. 421-422).

Likewise, the more introverted one becomes, i.e., moving the subjective into consciousness, the more extraversion moves into the unconscious. Extreme introverts sometimes become so withdrawn from the external world that they become reclusive. *"When people are introverted to the absolute extreme, they may be diagnosed as autistic or schizophrenic, and would live lives that in many respects were detached from everyday reality"* (Singer, 1994, p. 327). We find that on a daily basis, maintaining this delicate balance of attitude polarity requires extraverts to have some introverted time and introverts to have some extraverted time.

It is important to note that even strong extraverts need some time alone. If they are constantly interacting with people, they will eventually seek some "space." And likewise, strong introverts will eventually seek out someone with whom to briefly interact. We all live on the extraversion-introversion teeter-totter (Figure 4), moving between extraversion and introversion, varying the amount of time we spend in each based on our attitude Type. If we remain in our non-preferred mode too long we become uncomfortable.

Figure 4
Extraversion-Introversion Teeter-Totter

Jung's descriptions of the attitudes indicate that the strength of an external or internal focus can vary from one individual to another. In fact, it can vary in a single individual during the course of a day. I find it helpful to artificially categorize the degrees of attitude differentiation as low, medium and high. Individuals operating in the low or high (especially) ranges are prone to developing attitude-related neuroses as discussed above.

Summary

Jung's initial approach was to categorize human behavior based on the direction of psychic energy flow. He labeled energy flow outward toward the object as extraversion and inward toward the subject as introversion. These two "Types" provided the basis of his studies over a period of ten years. Table 5 presents a contrast between the extraverted and introverted attitude Types as well as estimates of the database percentage of each Type in the US adult population reported by Hammer and Mitchell (1996).

The attitude Types laid the foundation for Jung's psychological Type theory, but were not able to explain other wide variations in personality. Jung concluded that there had to be other factors that also played a role in guiding the flow of psychic energy. He expanded his theory to include four *function Types*.

Area	Extraverted Attitude Types	Introverted Attitude Types
Focus/ Energy Flow	The object The outer world People & things	The subject The inner world Ideas & thoughts
Prefers	Public Face-to-face encounters	Privacy Written communication
Values	Interaction Using outside resources	Reflection Being own best resource
Approach	Energetic & forceful Gregarious	Reserved & contemplative Introspective
Style	Thinks out loud Shows the world Shares space	Thinks before speaking Guards hidden side Territorial
US Population Percentage Estimate[12]	CAPT = 53% Myers = 65% SRI = 40% CPP = 46%	CAPT = 47% Myers = 35% SRI = 60% CPP = 54%

Table 5
Attitudes Contrast

---

[12] The percentages used in this Table are those reported by Hammer and Mitchell (1996). The following abbreviations are used in this Table: Center for Applications of Psychological Type (CAPT); Isabel Myers' High School Sample (Myers); Stanford Research Institute (SRI); Consulting Psychologists Press, Inc. (CPP).

Function Types

The Greek philosopher Empedocles attempted to impose order on the chaos of natural phenomena by dividing them into the four elements: earth, water, air and fire. It was above all the physicians of ancient times who applied this principle of order, in conjunction with the related doctrine of the four qualities, dry, moist, cold, warm, to human beings, and thus tried to reduce the bewildering diversity of mankind into orderly groups. Of these physicians one of the most important was Galen, whose use of these teachings influenced medical science and the treatment of the sick for seventeen hundred years. The very names of the Galenic temperaments betray their origin in the pathology of the four "humours". . . . melancholic . . . phlegmatic . . . sanguine . . . choleric. (Jung, 1976a, p. 542)

For the following discussion of Jung's function Types, I will use the same approach that Jung used in his writings: each function will be discussed as if it exists in a pure form—without the influence of the attitudes or the other functions. Thus, it might appear that only the extraverted form of the function is being discussed, essentially the same way it appears in Jung's work. In Chapters 4 and 5 the functions will be examined with their attitudes.

Jung's theory of psychological Types is based on psychic energy flow that manifests as a result of the interaction of three polarities, *attitude*, *perception* and *judgment*. These are polarities in that the attitudes of *extraversion* (E) and *introversion* (I) cannot be, according to Jung (1976a), in consciousness simultaneously. Likewise, the perceiving (irrational) functions, *Sensing* (S) and *iNtuiting* (N), cannot be used at the same time, nor can the judging (rational) functions of *Thinking* (T) and *Feeling* (F). Of the perceiving functions, Jung said, "*Sensation and intuition I call irrational functions, because they are both concerned simply with what happens and with actual or potential realities.*" And of the judging functions, "*Thinking and feeling, being discriminative functions, are rational*" (p. 553). The essence of psychological development is the differentiation[13] of the functions.

Jung (1976a) describes the functions as follows:

> *The four functions are somewhat like the four points of the compass; they are just as arbitrary and just as indispensable. Nothing prevents our*

---

[13]   Jung (1976a) defines differentiation as, "*the development of differences, the separation of parts from a whole. . . . So long as a function is so fused with one or more other functions— thinking with feeling, feeling with sensation, etc.—that it is unable to operate on its own, it is in an* archaic (q.v.) *condition* (p. 424).

> *shifting the cardinal points as many degrees as we*
> *like in one direction or the other, or giving them*
> *different names. But one thing I must confess: I*
> *would not for anything dispense with this compass*
> *on my psychological voyages of discovery.* (p.
> 541)

Figure 5
Jung's Compass

Jung (1976a) expands his definition of a function and gives
his iNtuiting, irrational justification for selecting the functions in
the following quotation.

> *By a psychological function I mean a particular*
> *form of psychic activity that remains the same in*
> *principle under varying conditions. . . . I can give*
> *no* a priori *reason for selecting these four as basic*
> *functions, and can only point out that this*
> *conception has shaped itself out of many years'*

experience. I distinguish these functions from one another because they cannot be related or reduced to one another. The principle of thinking, for instance, is absolutely different from the principle of feeling, and so forth. (pp. 436-437)

Hillman summarizes Jung's definition of a function as "*a relatively unified, relatively consistent and habitual pattern of performance which enjoys itself in its activity, a pattern that likes to be exercised* (von Franz & Hillman, 1971, p. 91).

Perceiving: The Monkey's Eye

In a classic psychological experiment in the 60's, Dr. Harry Harlow placed a cover over a cage containing a monkey to block out all external stimuli. Harlow wanted to determine the monkey's behavior in a visually deprived environment. He left a small hole in the cover to allow for observation of the monkey's behavior. To his surprise, what he saw when he looked through the hole was a monkey's eye looking out at him! The hole in the cover had become the monkey's *portal* to the outside world just as the perceiving functions (Sensing and iNtuiting) represent the psyche's portal for perceiving the external and internal worlds. Myers (1980) describes perceiving as "*the process of becoming aware of things, people, occurrences and ideas*" (p. 1). In other words, perceiving is the cognitive process of gathering information and bringing it into our consciousness. The perceiving polarity is divided into Sensing at one pole and iNtuiting at the other.

Sensing

Sensation is the psychological function that mediates the perception of a physical stimulus. It

is, therefore, identical with perception. . . .
Sensation is related not only to external stimuli but
to inner ones, i.e., to changes in the internal
organic processes. (Jung, 1976a, p. 461)

Sensing, the first response of the psyche to life, is the most basic and instinctual perceptive process of the psyche (Yabroff, 1990). It provides the infant with spontaneous, factual perceptual information about the realities of what is happening at the moment in its new environment. In fact, research suggests that the Sensing function is actually operational and storing information weeks before birth.

Sensing performs the psychological mediation between physical stimuli and conscious perceptions. In other words, Sensing is the process of collecting various forms of energy and converting, or translating, them into neural activity. Perceiving is the process of converting this neural activity into a form that can be recognized. Sensing makes use of the five primary senses of seeing, hearing, touching, smelling and tasting as well as the somatic senses (temperature and pain) and vestibular senses (information about the positions of body parts in relation to each other and the position of the head in space). The Sensing function, like the hole in the cage cover above, is our *portal to the world* through which *all* physical stimuli are perceived. Sensing collects data sequentially in that it processes data in the order it is received or as it happens.

As sensory information enters the psyche, an *experiential* memory is created that is based upon our interaction with the physical world. The experiential memory *"includes not only the sensory images we have accumulated over time and the practical knowledge which goes with them, but the memories of our subjective responses to those experiences"* (Newman, 1990, p. 11) and serves as a reference point with which future experiences can be compared. Newman refers to this memory as *common sense.*

There is evidence (Newman, 1990; Van der Hoop, 1939) to suggest that Sensing is significantly mediated by the Thinking and Feeling functions before stimuli are actually perceived in consciousness. This hypothesis will be explored in more detail in Chapter 6.

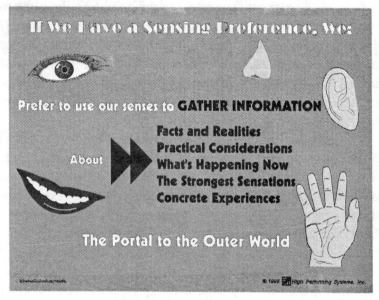

Figure 6
Sensing's General Character

Figure 6 provides a graphical representation[14] of the general characteristics of a Sensing Type. Sensing is the portal through which the world is accessed. The eye, mouth, hand, ear

---

[14] The character graphics for the four functions and eight function-attitudes that follow are taken from full color transparencies I specifically designed for use in presentations. Although they appear in black and white in this book, I will mention specific colors used on the transparencies in the brief descriptions. The colors were selected and arranged to create a specific effect characteristic of the particular function or function-attitude combination.

and nose represent the five senses and are displayed on a red background showing the vivid, three-dimensional world of the Sensing Type.

When Sensing is the dominant function in consciousness, behavior focuses on gathering information utilizing the bodily senses to collect data about facts, realities and what is specifically happening in the present and sensory experiences from the past (memory). Sensing allows us to be quick to see "what is," to grasp details and to be realistic in our approach. This Type is likely to prefer reality to fantasy and to be more specific and literal when speaking, writing or listening than when the other functions are active. At times, Sensing might prevent us from seeing the big picture or from being able to "see the forest for the trees." Sensing draws us toward problems for which we can find practical solutions and away from complex, theoretical or abstract situations.

iNtuiting

The other perceiving pole is iNtuiting, which is the perceptual function that creates, or generates, *insights, relationships* and *possibilities* from external and internal data. INtuiting involves the emergence from the unconscious of symbolic images, ideas and abstract experiences from an object that is not immediately present. Myers (1980) describes iNtuiting as the "*indirect perception by way of the unconscious* (p. 2)." INtuiting is very efficient at morphing and mediating perceptions in an unconscious way and can be described as an *ideational* process with *intellectual* overtones.

> *The primary function of intuition, however, is simply to transmit images, or perceptions of relations between things, which could not be transmitted by the other functions or only in a very*

roundabout way. (Jung, 1976a, p. 366)

> *While sensation is intimately tied to bodily experience (and emotion), intuition is predominantly a mental function, allowing for the perception, not of physical realities, but of symbolic images, ideas and abstractions. These contents of the intuitive process form the basis of mental experience. Intuition is, thus, an "intellectual" process.* (Newman, 1990, p. 13)

As iNtuiting perceives the unconscious manifestation of images, relationships and concepts, it stores them in a *symbolic* memory for later retrieval. Both Myers (1980) and Newman (1990) tie the act of communicating (reading, writing, listening and speaking) and the learning and use of mathematical concepts to the use of the symbolic memory. When using this type of memory, the time required for retrieval can range from instantaneous, to slow percolation in the unconscious, followed by an instant manifestation into consciousness—an "aha!" experience.

When iNtuiting is the dominant function in consciousness, behavior focuses on gathering information about meanings, possibilities and relationships. When using iNtuiting one tends to quickly see what could be, might be tripped up by details and uses the imagination actively and freely. Imagination is preferred to reality. INtuiting Types are generally abstract and visionary in talking, writing and listening and might be quick to "see the forest, but unable to see the trees." The iNtuiting function enables us to generate creative solutions to complicated or theoretical problems and to enjoy dealing with the complex. Conversely, there is a tendency to become impatient, ignore the practical and concrete and avoid thinking about the specifics necessary to carry out an assignment.

Figure 7 presents a graphical overview of the characteristics of a person who has a preference for iNtuiting. The background represents "space," indicating the vastness and unknown regions of this part of the psyche. The interconnected three-dimensional words represent the stream of ideas which, even though they might seem disparate to other function Types, are connected in the iNtuiting Type's mind.

Figure 7
iNtuiting's General Character

Table 6 provides a summary and contrast of the key features of the Sensing and iNtuiting functions.

Area	Sensing Function	iNtuiting Function
Focus	Facts Past/Present	Possibilities Relationships The future
Prefers	Facts	Hunches
Values	Reality	What could be
Approach	Methodical to completion	Skips from one activity to the next
Style	Views complex ideas as pieces	Views complex ideas as wholes
Memory	Experiential	Symbolic
US Population Percentage Estimate[15]	CAPT = 54% Myers = 68% SRI = 76% CPP = 68%	CAPT = 46% Myers = 32% SRI = 24% CPP = 32%

Table 6
Sensing - iNtuiting Contrasts

Judging: Evaluating What Is Perceived

While the perceiving functions infuse information into the psyche, the judging functions provide meaning, structure and valuation to perceived information. Myers (1980) describes judging as *"the process of coming to conclusions about what has been perceived"* (p. 1). Although the two judging functions are both rational, they travel along opposite paths during decision making and are prone to produce very different decisions based on the same set of perceived data.

---

[15] See footnote 12

Thinking

Thinking is a rational, judging process that structures and organizes experience and brings the contents of ideation into order. As the opposite pole of Feeling, Thinking judgment tends to be intellectual, analytical and impersonal. It uses a "right or wrong," "black or white," "logical or illogical" judging process. All data must fit into a logical categorical taxonomy. When using the Thinking function to make decisions, people prefer to decide things by considering abstract principles of right and wrong and applying these in an impersonal manner.

> *Intuition allows us to directly perceive and respond to these images, to intuitively comprehend the world of the symbolic and abstract. Thinking takes these half-formed ideas and places them within an organized system of thought, accepting or rejecting them, relating them to existing knowledge, and allowing for their expression in a logical and consistent manner.* (Newman, 1990, p. 7)

Thinking judgments tend to be somewhat slower than Feeling judgments because of a need to have more information. Thinking links the past, present and future together in a cause-and-effect relationship. To do this often requires more analysis, more information and, consequently, more time to reach a decision. Although Thinking processes data sequentially, it uses an ordinal sequence—a specific logical sequence such as 1, 2, 3, etc.—rather than the occurrence sequence (as it happens) used by Sensing.

The Thinking function builds an *intellectual* memory based on the logical organization and analysis of facts, concepts and relationships (Newman, 1990). Intellectual memory is influenced by the environment and introspective reflection. Thinking critiques information creating intellectual knowledge domains (memory).

When Thinking is in control of consciousness, people are often unaware of their emotions or do not show them easily. They tend to be uncomfortable when dealing with other people's emotions and, perhaps, hurt other people's feelings unknowingly. This leads to impersonal decision making and sometimes to giving insufficient attention to other people's wishes. Information is logically organized and impersonally analyzed. There is a deliberate effort by Thinking Types to keep their own and others' emotions out of decisions that are being made. The analytically oriented Thinking Type responds more to data than to people, although being treated fairly by others is very important.

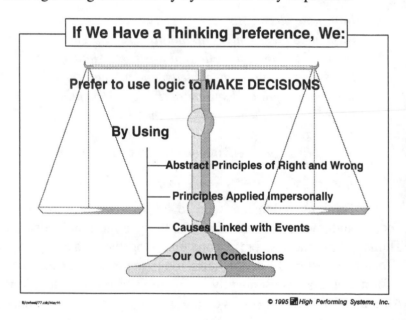

If We Have a Thinking Preference, We:

Prefer to use logic to MAKE DECISIONS

By Using

— Abstract Principles of Right and Wrong

— Principles Applied Impersonally

— Causes Linked with Events

— Our Own Conclusions

Figure 8
Thinking's General Character

Figure 8 is a graphical overview of common characteristics of someone who has a preference for Thinking. It is black and white, representing the Thinking Type's black or white approach to judgment, and has a set of scales in the background indicating impersonal decision making and trusting their own conclusions. The text is presented in Thinking's logical, structured format.

I often use an analogy to describe Thinking Types as being like m&m's®[16]—they have a hard candy shell on the outside, but on the inside they are like milk chocolate. Just like Feeling Types, Thinking Types have feelings and care about people.

Feeling

> *Feeling . . . is an entirely* subjective *process, which may be in every respect independent of external stimuli, though it allies itself with every sensation. Even an "indifferent" sensation possesses a feeling-tone, namely that of indifference, which again expresses some sort of valuation. Hence, feeling is a kind of* judgment, *differing from intellectual judgment in that its aim is not to establish conceptual relations but to set up a subjective criterion of acceptance or rejection. Valuation by feeling extends to every content of consciousness, of whatever kind it may be.* (Jung, 1976a, p. 434)

The Feeling function, the other half of the judging polarity, is perhaps the least understood of all the functions and attitudes. Jung (1976a) says, *"The intellect proves incapable of formulating the real nature of feeling in conceptual terms, since thinking belongs to a category incommensurable with feeling. . . . That being so, it is impossible . . . to reproduce the specific character*

---

[16] m&m's® is a registered trademark of Mars, Incorporated.

of feeling at all adequately" (p. 435-436). Mattoon (1981) elaborates further on what Feeling is not when she states, *"The phrase 'It feels soft (or hard),' expresses what Jung called sensation; 'I have a feeling that something is going to happen,' reflects intuition; and 'I feel depressed,' refers to emotion. Feeling must be distinguished from emotion especially"* (p. 64). Affect[17] can be associated with the Feeling function, but they are not one and the same. Feeling can be completely devoid of affect.

Feeling is a rational judging process that can quickly establish an attitude of value toward people, events and things. The Feeling process is very dynamic, ordering and re-ordering information. It structures and evaluates all experiences. Everything is assigned a value. The Feeling process, unlike Thinking, recognizes shades of gray. It connects the internal world to the external world and the external world to the internal world.

Hillman states that *"through the feeling function we appreciate a situation, a person, an object, a moment, in terms of value. A prerequisite for feeling is therefore a structure of feeling memory, a set of values, to which the event can be related"* (von Franz & Hillman, 1971, p. 90). Newman (1990) labels this *affective* memory. Affective memory is regulated by and provides influence on the Feeling function and is both visual and experiential. Unlike Thinking, Feeling is a non-intellectual process that establishes and shapes a person's values. It builds up over time, based on past and present experiences, and centers around the external world (object). It can be strongly influenced by the societal norms of the environment and reflection. "Feeling

---

[17] *Affect tends to contaminate or distort each of the functions: we can't think straight when we are mad; happiness colors the way we perceive things and people; we can't properly evaluate what something is worth to us when we're upset; and possibilities dry up when we're depressed.* (Sharp, 1987, p. 18)

moments" are chained together over time. When the affective memory is evoked, *events seem to be happening in real-time.*

Although affective memory is built up over time, Feeling judgments are usually made very quickly. Feeling judgments are a little slower than the perceiving functions because Feeling must rationally organize perceptions and then judge them. The more differentiated the Feeling function, however, the more time it takes to make a decision. The Feeling function has a sense of timing and tact that makes it incompatible with the rationale of the Thinking function.

When consciousness is under the dominant influence of the Feeling function, people are in touch with their emotions and values and are able to express them appropriately. They tend to be aware of and responsive to other people's emotions and values and enjoy pleasing people, even in unimportant things. Feeling Types prefer to live and work in harmonious settings and their decisions are often influenced by their own or others' personal likes and dislikes. They seem to need personal praise frequently and are constantly seeking it. It is important for Feeling Types to establish and maintain harmonious relationships with others, and personal praise is a measure of how successful they are in a relationship whether it is personal or professional. This high need for praise can sometimes cause the Feeling Type to have difficulty keeping "people considerations" in perspective when making decisions. One result of this is a tendency to overcommit themselves rather than saying "no."

Figure 9 provides a graphical overview of the general characteristics of a Feeling Type. A yellow background is used to represent a peaceful environment and the gradational color change represents degrees of valuation—in contrast to Thinking's black or white logic. The house, family, children, animals and flowers indicate Feeling's strong association with people, animals and societal norms.

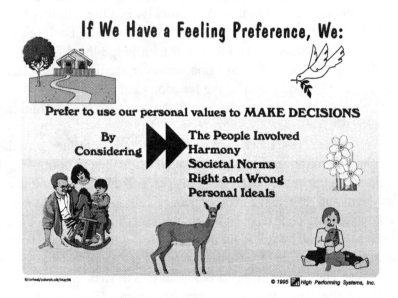

Figure 9
Feeling's General Character

Table 7 provides a summary of key judging factors and a contrast of the Thinking and Feeling functions.

Area	Thinking Function	Feeling Function
Focus	Objective criteria	Subjective criteria
Prefers	Principles	Values
Values	Policies/Laws Justice Logic	Humaneness Harmony Subjectivity
Approach	Impersonal Black or white Standards Analytical Naming Categorizing	Personal Shades of gray Values Sympathetic Determining worth Relating
Style	Businesslike	Warm & friendly
Memory	Intellectual	Affective
US Population Percentage Estimates[18]	CAPT = 42% Myers = 48% SRI = 50% CPP = 53%	CAPT = 58% Myers = 52% SRI = 50% CPP = 47%

Table 7
Thinking - Feeling Contrast

The memory domain for each of the four functions is summarized in Table 8 and provides descriptive words for each memory process.

---

[18] See footnote 12

Experiential Memory **S**	Symbolic Memory **N**
Sensory images Sensory responses Subjective responses Linear, nominal Common sense	Images Interconnectedness Visual Nonlinear Creative
Intellectual Memory **T**	Affective Memory **F**
Logic Cause & effect Taxonomies Linear, sequential Intellect	Values Societal norms Chained "moments" Nonlinear Affect

Table 8
Functional Memory Summary

Operating Modes

Scattered throughout Jung's writings are vague references to the functional *operating modes: active* and *passive; concrete* and *abstract*. One of Jung's goals was to gain control over the functions to the degree that he could call a function into consciousness and use it in a differentiated manner at will. The close similarity of the operating modes predisposes them for confusion. What follows is an attempt to consolidate and give a sense of clarity to some of his thoughts about these modes. The fainthearted might want to skip this section.

Active-Passive. Jung (1976a) describes an active and passive use of the attitudes and functions. The active use of an attitude or function requires an *act of will*, a conscious, directed use of the attitude or function in a differentiated manner. Jung (1976a) states that "*Extraversion is* active *when it is intentional*" (p. 427) and introversion "*is* active *when the subject* [person] *voluntarily shuts himself off from the object*" (p. 453).

The four functions can also be used in an active manner. When this occurs, the function is consciously evoked, person-driven and directed. Feeling, for example, when used in the active mode, transfers or assigns value from the internal world to an object in the external world. This is an "*intentional valuation of the content in accordance with feeling and not in accordance with the intellect. . . . a directed function, an act of will. . . . loving as opposed to being in love*" (Jung, 1976a, p. 436).

When operating in the passive mode, attitudes and functions lack direction and are reactive, controlled by content and closely intermingled with other functions. When extraversion is passive, "*the object compels it, i.e., when the object attracts the subject's* [person's] *interest of its own accord, even against his will*" (Jung, 1976a, p. 427). When introversion is passive, "*he is unable to restore to the object the libido* [psychic energy] *streaming back from it*" (p. 453).

For example, when passive Feeling is undirected it "*allows itself to be attracted or excited by a particular content, which then forces the feelings of the subject* [person] *to participate* (Jung, 1976a, p. 436). In this mode Feeling is undirected and intermingled with the other functions, especially iNtuiting. Jung refers to undirected Feeling as Feeling iNtuiting.

Abstract-Concrete. The functions can operate in an abstract[19] or concrete mode. The abstract mode is a highly

---

[19] Jung (1976a, p. 409) describes abstract as "*the drawing out or singling out of a content (a meaning, a general characteristic, etc.) from a context made up of other elements whose combination into a whole is something unique or individual and therefore cannot be compared to anything*

differentiated use of the function in a directed manner (act of will) that is consciously evoked with an *awareness* of the psycho-energic process. The product produced by this use tends to be irrepresentable. Abstract Feeling allows the individual to rise above the content being evaluated. The contents are arranged based on *universal* and objective values. The more abstract the Feeling function, the more universal the valuation.

The concrete mode is a reactive, primitive and undifferentiated use of a function of which the subject is *unaware*. For example, concrete Feeling is "simple Feeling"— Feeling that is intermingled with the other functions producing a jumble of emotions and reactions, but primarily driven and controlled by Sensing. The more concrete the use, the more subjective and personal are the valuations (judgments) made by the Feeling function. In a highly concrete mode the person might not be able to distinguish between internal feelings and the sensed object (person, place, thing, etc.)—the object becomes synonymous with the feeling. The operating modes are summarized in Table 9.

---

else." Concrete means *"grown together. A concretely thought concept is one that has coalesced with other concepts*" (p. 420). MBTI users should note that Jung uses abstract and concrete a little differently than they tend to be used in MBTI Type training and discussions.

Active	Passive
Act of will	Reactive
Allows for differentiation	Intermingled
Allows for Type development	Controlled by content
	An occurrence
Person-driven	Lacks direction
Consciously evoked	Irrational
Voluntary	
Abstract	**Concrete**
Directed/Act of will	Reactive
Detached from other functions	Mixed with other functions
	Representable
Irrepresentable	Unaware
Awareness of psycho-energic process	Holistic
	Primitive
Focused on a part	Irrational
Consciously evoked	

Table 9
Operating Modes Summary

Summary

Through his observations and studies, Jung found that the functions and attitudes did not operate independently but combined to produce a set of eight distinguishable *function-attitudes*. Each of these will be discussed in following chapters.

The Perceiving Function-Attitudes

After Jung conceived of his typology based on the extraversion-introversion polarity, he went through a ten-year period of doubting these early formulations. . . . To achieve the subtlety and refinement which Jung felt appropriate to his observations on personality differences, he added the four basic functions, which he termed sensation, intuition, thinking and feeling, and concluded that "strictly speaking, there are no introverts and extraverts pure and simple, but only introverted and extraverted function-types." (Spoto, 1995, p. 42)

The functions (Sensing, iNtuiting, Thinking & Feeling) combine with the attitudes (extraversion & introversion) to form eight function-attitude Types, e.g., extraverted Sensing[20], as shown in Table 10.

Function	Attitude	Function-Attitude Type
Sensing	Extraverted	Extraverted Sensing (S_e)
	Introverted	Introverted Sensing (S_i)
iNtuiting	Extraverted	Extraverted iNtuiting (N_e)
	Introverted	Introverted iNtuiting (N_i)
Thinking	Extraverted	Extraverted Thinking (T_e)
	Introverted	Introverted Thinking (T_i)
Feeling	Extraverted	Extraverted Feeling (F_e)
	Introverted	Introverted Feeling (F_i)

Table 10
Function-Attitude Types

As with the attitude Types and the function Types, the following discussion will proceed as if the function-attitude Types are pure and uninfluenced by interaction with the other function-attitudes. The descriptions are also presented in the context of a dominant function-attitude Type. That is, when a function-attitude is discussed, it will be as if it has full control of the person without influence from the other functions. When reading about your own dominant function-attitude, you will experience the influence of your auxiliary function. For example, although both INFJs and INTJs will identify strongly with the introverted iNtuiting Type,

---

[20] From this point forward a shorthand will be used to represent the function-attitude combinations. The function will be represented by a capital letter and the associated attitude by a lower case subscript, e.g., extraverted Sensing is S_e.

they might find themselves wanting to add to or delete from the description because of the influence of their T or F auxiliary. Other Types might have a similar experience.

The descriptions presented here represent a synthesis of my observations, Jung's writings and my interpretations of his writings, as well as the work of Beebe (personal communication, 1996), Hartzler (personal communication, 1996), Marshall (personal communication, 1996), Myers (1980), Quenk (1993), Sharp (1987), Spoto (1995) and others. It is not intended to be the final word, but rather a quick summary for those who want to have a basic understanding of the function-attitude Types but are not interested in becoming Jungian scholars.

At the beginning of each section, a Table will show the two MBTI Types that have a particular function-attitude in the dominant role and the two Types that have it in the auxiliary role. The rationale for this is that many characteristics of the dominant form will be visible when the function-attitude appears in the extraverted auxiliary form, even though another function-attitude is dominant. For example, you will notice that an ISTP (auxiliary extraverted Sensing) exhibits some of the same characteristics as an ESTP (dominant extraverted Sensing) because Sensing is extraverted in both cases and, consequently, easily observable. Introverted auxiliary Types will also be shown even though the effect is often difficult to observe.

As you read through the Type descriptions, remember that Jung said the most difficult Type to understand was not your opposite (e.g., extraverted Thinking vs. introverted Feeling), but rather the Type with the same function and the opposite attitude, e.g., extraverted Thinking vs. introverted Thinking.

The discussion of each function-attitude will be formatted into four sections: the function-attitude *process, behavior, memory* and *in the grip.* The process section will address the basic activity of the function-attitude—how it works. The behavior section will present an overview of the general observable behavior of this

Type from a purist perspective. Memory will be addressed from the perspective of the contribution of the function-attitude to the appropriate memory domain. The "in the grip"[21] section will give an overview of common behaviors of the function-attitude when it manifests as an out-of-control inferior function-attitude, temporarily taking over consciousness. This is commonly referred to in Jungian and Myers-Briggs circles as being "in the grip" of the inferior. Quenk (1993) states that

> *In the grip of your inferior, you don't become a mature, well-functioning opposite type, since your experience and facility with your least preferred function is relatively limited. So you turn into a rather sorry example of your opposite.* (p. 51)

The eruption of the inferior can occur whenever there is a "lowering of our general level of consciousness." Quenk (1993) identifies the most common *triggers* that significantly increase the probability of in the grip experiences as fatigue, illness, stress and mind-altering drugs (e.g., alcohol).

A function-attitude exercise using m&m's is included in the Appendix. It is recommended that you complete this exercise yourself before proceeding as an experiential means of gaining a deeper understanding of the function-attitudes.

---

[21] The best and most complete treatment of "in the grip" experiences from a psychological Type (Myers-Briggs) perspective is Dr. Naomi L. Quenk's 1993 book, *Beside Ourselves*, published by CPP Books, Palo Alto, California. The temperament complement is Dr. Eve Delunas' 1992 book, *Survival Games Personalities Play*, published by Sunflower, Inc., Carmel, California.

Perceiving Function-Attitudes

The perceiving functions (S & N) combine with the attitudes (E & I) to form four perceiving function-attitude Types, S_e, S_i, N_e and N_i as shown in Figure 10. Each will be discussed in turn.

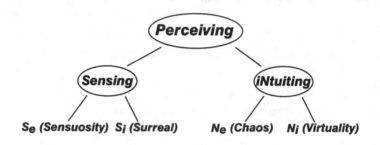

Figure 10
Perceiving Function-Attitudes

You will note that along with each function-attitude Type is an accompanying *image* label (Table 11). These labels, "*sensuosity*," "*surreal*," "*chaos*" and "*virtuality*" provide a metaphorical image of the "world" in which a particular function-attitude Type lives. I have found these "extra" descriptions to be helpful in the quest to understand Types other than our own—and, in some cases, our own.

F-A	Image	Abstraction
S_e	Sensuosity	A strong drive for sensory gratification that results in a fusion with the reality of the moment, experienced in extreme 3-D, digitized, Dolby® Surround Sound™. Not just living in the present, but *being* the present.
S_i	Surreal	The production and experience of incongruous imagery or dreamlike reality that can be so vivid that it seems "real."
N_e	Chaos	A state of seemingly unorganized polyphasic thoughts and behaviors resembling William James' (1890) *stream of consciousness*.
N_i	Virtuality	A world of indescribable images and potentialities where everything is possible, even the most bizarre and paradoxical combinations.

Table 11
Perceiving Function-Attitudes Abstractions

Extraverted Sensing Types (S$_e$): "Sensuosity"[22]

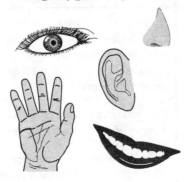

> *Kennedy is a man completely and vigorously
> engaged in events of the moment. Thus he regards
> his past acts as more or less irrelevant prologue;
> his future acts as something to be determined
> under future circumstances. One could talk to him
> all day and be unable to say what his attitude
> toward business will be, because what he says or
> thinks on that day has a bearing only on the effect
> he is trying to achieve that day.* (Louis Banks,
> 1987[23])

When combined with the extraverted attitude, dominant
Sensing forms the extraverted Sensing Type. This Type is

---

[22] As you read the extraverted Type descriptions you will notice that
they sound similar to descriptions of the "four" functions as described in basic
MBTI classes. I believe this is the case because when we "hear" a function in
action (conversation, etc.), we hear its extraverted form.

[23] Quoted in Donovan, 1987.

exemplified by John F. Kennedy[24] and his "live-in-the-moment" lifestyle. Other historical S_e figures include General George S. Patton, Jr., the grasshopper from "The Ant and the Grasshopper" fable and "Maverick" in the popular movie *Top Gun*®.

Dominant Function-Attitude	MBTI Types with S_e Dominant	MBTI Types with S_e Auxiliary
S_e	ESTP ESFP	ISTP ISFP

Table 12
Extraverted Sensing Types

Jung (1976a), in describing the S_e, states:

No other human type can equal the extraverted sensation type in realism. His sense for objective facts is extraordinarily developed. His life is an accumulation of actual experiences of concrete objects, and the more pronounced his type, the less use does he make of his experience. In certain cases the events of his life hardly deserve the name

---

[24] Along with each function-attitude I will present one or more historical examples of that function-attitude. These people were chosen based on my "best guess" from reviewing their biographies, philosophies and accounts of their behavior. As with all typo-historical guesses, the person's Type has not been validated; thus logical cases could be made (and in some cases have been made) that these individuals are of a different Type. The purpose for their inclusion here is not to stimulate debate, but rather to give historical behavioral examples of the kinds of effects that are characteristic of a particular function-attitude Type.

*"experience" at all. What he experiences serves at
most as a guide to fresh sensations; anything new
that comes within range of his interest is acquired
by way of sensation and has to serve as ends.* (p.
363)

Extraverted Sensing enables us to perceive, in a relatively
uncategorized fashion, and record factual data about objective
(external) stimuli. The S_e lives in a *sensory* world where, barring
a physical disability, everything within the range of human
perception is perceived. When Sensing takes on the extraverted
attitude (S_e) the person experiences an expanded range and depth
of colors, tastes, touches, sounds and smells relative to other
Types. S_e creates a heightened sensitivity of the senses. It is as if
everything is in three-dimensional, digitized, Dolby® Surround
Sound™. Amid this sensuous environment, life is experienced as
a "rush."

As a soldier in Vietnam, I developed my inferior function,
S_e, to the degree that when asleep in the jungle, if the bugs stopped
chirping anywhere around me I woke up. Bugs get quiet when
something large, like a person, moves close to them. The *absence*
of noise in any direction became an alarm clock! My sense of
smell developed to the point that I could often smell people (the
enemy) hiding in ambush a hundred meters away. On a totally
dark night, I have been able to "feel" another person's movement
through the air much as a shark feels the vibrations of its prey in
the water.

Like a bug drawn to a bright light, the S_e is drawn to the
strongest sensation, then the next, then the next and so on. An
example is a scene from *The Sound of Music*© when Maria first
arrives at the von Trapp house. Upon entering the house she finds
the vast array of stimuli (huge staircases, enormous rooms,
number of children, whistles, etc.) overpowering and is repeatedly
drawn from one stimulus to another. S_es focus on the physical

facts of their environment and tend to be very literal when speaking or interpreting conversation. They don't pay much attention to anything that is not concrete, such as hunches, fantasies, etc. Whatever comes from the subjective is suspect.

This Type "sees" the minute details that elude the rest of the world. Once I showed my brother a letter I had received from a company trying to sell me something. He glanced at it, handed it back to me and said, "I would be embarrassed to send out a letter like that." I told him that I thought it was a good marketing letter. He agreed that the content was fine, but added, "Look at the fonts. The edges are not smooth. You would think that a company as great as that letter makes it seem could afford a good printer." With effort, I was able to see that the edges on some of the fonts were not perfectly smooth. S_es want and need the specifics and details of everything with which they come in contact.

Figure 11
Extraverted Sensing's Character

The S_e graphic (Figure 11) has a bright red, three-dimensional background spanned by a rainbow, indicating the vividness and spacial qualities of this Type; the skydiver represents the action-oriented rush of life. This detailed drawing represents the level of detail S_es perceive. The power of strong sensations to draw the S_e's attention is represented by the light bulb surrounded by bugs. The word "sensuosity" is displayed between the writing and the rainbow.

Behavior. Extraverted Sensors see and experience everything. They do not live just in the present, *they are part of it.* Several years ago while attending a social function, I slipped into the room where the World Series was playing on T.V. After about a minute, a second person came in and a third arrived about twenty seconds later asking for the score. I said, "Three to nothing, Cardinals." The second man, who had been in the room only about twenty seconds longer than the third said, "It's three to nothing Cardinals; bottom of the second; the count is two and two. There's one out; Jones is on base, . . ." and continued to amaze us with the amount of detail he had gleaned in a short period of time.

With the energy flow directed toward the external world, the S_e tends to respond instinctively and reflexively to the surroundings. They operate in *real-time* and produce observable, spontaneous responses closely mediated by the Thinking and Feeling functions. The behavior of the S_e is outgoing, action oriented and lively. They focus on the facts and demonstrate little understanding of or patience for the complex or theoretical. They prefer to make their own rules and not to be boxed in by the rules of others. The S_e seeks out action, activity, excitement and the strongest stimuli available. When their interests are focused artistically, they have the ability to be innovative[25] in the use of

---

[25] I make a distinction between innovation and creativity. As used in this book, innovation means finding new ways to use existing things. Creativity is defined as developing something that did not exist previously.

their time and physical skills.

They are often proficient navigators and, although they might appear disorganized, they rarely lose things. I had a client (ESTP) whose desk always looked as if a large trash can had been emptied on it. One day I asked him if he had a copy of a memo that had been written six weeks earlier. He walked to his desk, lifted up the top two-thirds of a large, disorganized pile of papers and pulled out the memo. He then said to me, "It might look disorganized, but I know where everything is."

Memory. Extraverted Sensing feeds "raw," uncategorized objective (external) experiences into *experiential* memory. Newman (1990) defines experiential memory as *"the sum total of previous sensation-mediated experiences. It is the storehouse of all experiences in dealing with the physical world"* (p. 10). The S_e data goes into memory just as it occurs.

In the Grip. When the S_e's inferior function, introverted iNtuiting, takes control, it manifests in a primitive, archaic form of N_i. Jung (1976a) states that when the inferior N_i takes over,

> *Repressed intuitions begin to assert themselves in the form of projections. The wildest suspicions arise. . . . More acute cases develop every sort of phobia, and, in particular, compulsion symptoms. . . . contents have a markedly unreal character. . . [and] rest on the most absurd assumptions, in complete contrast to the conscious sense of reality. . . . reason turns into hair-splitting pedantry, morality into dreary moralizing . . . religion into ridiculous superstition, and intuition . . . into meddlesome officiousness.* (p. 365)

The normally factual, data-based, outgoing, down-to-earth S_es may suddenly become mystical, experiencing a world of negative premonitions, fear of the future, anxiety, depression and a seeming inability to control what is happening around them. This perceived loss of control often leads to depression and sometimes just "giving up."

Introverted Sensing Types (S$_i$): "Surreal"

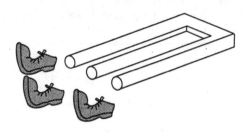

*After losing one of my rubber boots I bought
another pair. I kept the remaining boot of the first
pair in case I lost another one. The three of them
were sitting together inside my back door when a
friend came over to visit. Later, as we were
talking, I mentioned losing one of my boots and
that I now had three. My friend said that he
noticed the three boots sitting together when he
entered the door and visualized me in his mind
with three legs—which did not seem odd to him at
the time!* (John Beebe, 1996[26])

Stories like this one about Dr. Beebe's friend are not
unusual for S$_i$s. They live in an inner, *surreal* world where, in
extreme cases, it is difficult to discern internal from external
"reality." In this surreal world, the S$_i$ Type experiences
incongruous energies and vivid, dream-like realities. The surreal

---

[26] When sharing the image label concept with Dr. John Beebe after the
Bay Area (San Francisco) APT meeting in January of 1996, he had an "aha!"
experience and related this event which had recently occurred with his friend.

world of the S_i is distinguished from that of the N_i in that it is based on actual recalled experiences rather than imagination.

Dominant Function-Attitude	MBTI Types with S_i Dominant	MBTI Types with S_i Auxiliary
S_i	ISTJ ISFJ	ESTJ ESFJ

Table 13
Introverted Sensing MBTI Types

The introverted Sensing Types experience strong subjective sensations—so strong that the brain might not distinguish between a recalled sensory experience and external "reality." For example, recall when you or someone else slowly scraped fingernails across a chalkboard. If you are like most people, just the thought of fingernails scraping a chalkboard produces the same physiological responses (goose bumps, cold chills, etc.) as if it were actually happening. To hear someone talk about eating a lemon tends to produce salivation and sour facial expressions in many people. Other events such as the attack on Pearl Harbor, John F. Kennedy's assassination or the Challenger explosion still evoke powerful memories years, even decades, later. These events are retrieved through introverted Sensing.

S_i focuses psychic energy on past associations and experiences and on the background of objects. It produces strong subjective sensations and experiences capable of creating a surreal effect. Sensory experiences are categorized and stored for evaluating future experiences. The S_i Type absorbs every detail of a situation.

Emma Jung (Carl Jung's wife), an S_i Type, described herself as a highly sensitized photographic plate (von Franz & Hillman, 1971). She said that when someone entered a room, she noticed everything about the person, including hair, expression, pace, clothes, how the person walked, etc., as if a picture had been taken of the person producing a very precise impression. She further elaborated on the S_i process describing it as:

> *though a stone fell into deep water: the impression falls deeper and deeper and sinks in. Outwardly, the introverted sensation type looks utterly stupid. He just sits and stares, and you do not know what is going on within him. He looks like a piece of wood with no reaction at all—unless he reacts with one of the auxiliary functions, thinking or feeling. But inwardly the impression is being absorbed.* (p. 34)

The S_i, sitting quietly, covertly records very precisely both extraverted and introverted sensory experiences and constantly compares past and present sensations.

The S_i is drawn to the subjective (internal world) and is internally focused. A stimulus provided by the external world is quickly replaced by an internal sensation evoked by the external stimulus. The subjectivity (internal focus) of this Type creates an internal reality mediated by Thinking, Feeling, past associations and experiences. Responses tend to be hidden from others' view, making it difficult to determine the strength or type of response evoked by a stimulus object in the S_i Type; consequently, their behavior tends to be difficult to predict. There appears to be no direct relationship between the strength of the external stimulus and the strength of the internal response evoked in the person. The external stimulus evokes an internal sensation that, once evoked, becomes surreal and takes on a character, direction and strength of its own. This all happens in real-time and is focused on the immediate, internal experience. The response tends to come about somewhat slowly and cautiously as it percolates in the psyche.

Van der Hoop (1939) postulates that the S_i Type experiences strong visceral and emotional associations with sensory perceptions. Allen Marshall (1994) also suggests that the S_i's visceral and emotional responses to new experiences tend to produce a highly conserving Type whose *"reliance on the subjective impressions can also make one believe that there is only one right way to do something, and that is the way I believe it should be done (because other ways create homoeostatic imbalance within an S_i)."* If S_i has a strong visceral tie to perceptions, then it should also have an impact on awareness of bodily sensations.

Behavior. In describing the behavior of the S_i Types, one needs to focus on their responses to the immediate situation—"living the moment." They experience a rush of internal sensations, although it might not be apparent to onlookers. On the outside they appear calm, passive, rational and in control. It might appear as if they are not reacting to events around them when, in reality, on the inside there is a flurry of activity taking place as they process the internal sensations evoked by the external stimuli. They might seem difficult to get to know because they tend to hold their thoughts (connecting the present to the past through stored impressions) and emotions inside.

S_is behave as if they believe things will always be the way they are this moment, with little prediction or belief in the future or in change. They might also respond slowly to events happening around them; for example, a joke might be laughed at later in the day. This apparent "slowness" might cause others to perceive them as inferior or not as quick as the S_e Types who respond immediately to everything. At times, S_i Types might believe they are at a disadvantage to those around them and that bad things and events tend to happen just to them. For example, they always pick the wrong line, get onions on their hamburgers when they ask for no onions, etc. Murphy's Law was probably written by an S_i.

Memory. Introverted Sensing feeds experiential memory by providing subjective, visceral and emotional experiences and the categorization of sensory data. S_i creates and records in memory an instinctual response to external and internal stimuli. Internal responses and sensations are organized and stored in this memory, providing a mechanism for the S_i to recall experiences and responses from the past. This type of memory tends to be eidetic (extraordinarily vivid, sometimes referred to as photographic memory). For example, we can recall that m&m's have chocolate on the inside and how different types of m&m's smelled, tasted or sounded. A precise, organized and lasting memory of events is created by S_i. The data retrieval process tends to be a sequential search. When trying to match a name to a face the S_i tends to begin the search with names beginning with "A," then "B," etc.

In workshops lasting two or more days, I often move the participants' name tents to different locations around the table for the beginning of the second day to encourage, among other things, interaction with different participants. In one particular workshop, I had finished the first day with a discussion of the differences among the functions. That evening I moved the name tents around. The next morning when the participants began to arrive in the meeting room, Bill (the only S_i in the group) stopped in the middle of the doorway and commented, "You've moved all the name tents to different places!" It was as if he had made a photograph of the room before he left the evening before and was comparing the "new" room arrangement to it. Most participants returned to their original seats (especially iNtuiting Types who actually sat behind someone else's name tent and did not notice until it was pointed out). The S_i is an astute observer who sees and remembers the physical world in detail.

In the Grip. The inferior process for the S_i Type is extraverted iNtuiting. N_e causes the S_i to focus on the background of events taking place. Numerous possibilities are generated from the underworld of the inferior form of N_e.

> *If you try to force him to assimilate intuition too quickly, he gets symptoms of giddiness or sea sickness. He feels carried away from the solid ground of reality, and because he is so stuck there, he gets actual symptoms of sea sickness.* (von Franz & Hillman, 1971, p. 36)

S_is may be so drawn to the subjective mythological world that they might at times actually lose the ability to distinguish between reality and the surreal. The tendency under this condition is to focus on negative possibilities and attach symbolic meanings to "things" in the external world. This can lead to compulsive neurosis with hysterical features masked by symptoms of exhaustion and a feeling of "no way out" of the stressful situation.

The introverted Sensing graphic (Figure 12) has a red, three-dimensional background with fuzzy edges depicting the surreal, dreamlike world of the S_i. The man remembering the pie is experiencing the physiological responses of eating a pie from the past. The lemon with juice dripping from it is another example of how S_i can recall an experience so strongly and realistically that the body cannot recognize the difference—in this case producing a salivation response. The three-pronged illusion represents another example of a surreal effect. The dragon and knight represent the predisposition to create internal myths that may become the S$_i$'s perception of "reality." The word "surreal" is burned[27] across the background as if it had been written on paper with lemon juice, then heated.

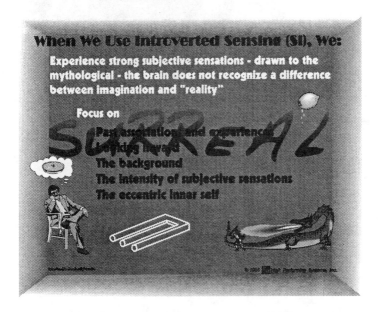

Figure 12
Introverted Sensing's Character

---

[27] An effective way of writing "secret messages" when I was a child was to write with lemon juice. When the juice dried it was invisible. The receiver of the message would hold the paper above a lighted candle and the heat would cause the message to appear.

Extraverted iNtuiting Types (N$_e$): "Chaos"

> *Chaos . . . those nonrandom complicated motions that exhibit a very rapid growth of errors that, despite perfect determinism, inhibits any pragmatic ability to render accurate long-term prediction.* (Peitgen, Jurgens & Saupe, 1992, p. 6)

Many scientists say that the three greatest scientific accomplishments of the 20th century are the *new sciences:* relativity, quantum mechanics and chaos theory. Mitchell Feigenbaum, one of the developers of chaos theory, defines chaos technically in the quote above. Chaos theory attempts to explain the unpredictability of actions in the real world such as the apparently random motions of a stick floating down a stream or the fractal[28] shown above. The N$_e$s appear (to the non-N$_e$s) to be in chaos and exhibit apparently random, unpredictable behavior. Chaos can be thought of as a process or a transformation rather

---

[28] The Figure at the beginning of this section is a portion of a fractal known as a Mandelbrot set, named after its creator, Benoit Mandelbrot. It is computed from a very simple-looking mathematical equation and results in the most complex mathematical figure known.

than something that *is*. Paradoxically, chaos is deterministic, i.e., generated by a set of fixed rules which do not change. Even though N_es might appear to be totally out of control, their random behavior or randomness is generated by an implicit set of extraverted iNtuiting rules.

Dominant Function-Attitude	MBTI Types with N_e Dominant	MBTI Types with N_e Auxiliary
N_e	ENTP ENFP	INTP INFP

Table 14
Extraverted iNtuiting MBTI Types

The extraverted iNtuiting Type lives in a world of ideas, a stream of consciousness reminiscent of William James. The N_e attitude of expectancy creates a constant searching for the widest range of possibilities, resulting in the person being easily distracted and appearing to be at the edge of *chaos*. Thus, the N_e becomes suffocated by stability. The primary purpose of N_e is to perceive behind-the-scenes aspects not observable by Sensing. The N_e's perception involves possibility-seeking using sensations as starting points for an intellectual process of seeing through or behind the object. N_es quickly comprehend the complex and read between the lines in interpersonal interactions.

Sharp (1987) says:

In the extravert, where intuition is oriented toward things and other people, there is an extraordinary ability to sense what is going on behind the scenes, under the surface; it "sees through" the outer layer. Where the comparatively mundane

> *perception of the sensation type sees "a thing" or*
> *"a person," the intuitive sees its soul.* (p. 59)

Driven by external conditions, N_es can quickly change directions, like a stick in a stream, and adapt to the environment.

Behavior. The behavior of the N_e is marked by high enthusiasm and a passion for new projects, new experiences and new challenges. They are innovative entrepreneurs and visionaries, constantly generating new ideas and *creative* ways of doing things. Their passion for new ideas and active imagination gives them a quick wit, usually with a well-developed vocabulary and a flair for dramatics. Learning foreign languages tends to come easily for N_es.

Today's focus might become a turning point in the N_e's life. Tomorrow, however, this Type might experience a new turning point and turn again. They want to do everything, to fully engage and explore all the possibilities in the environment. Their exuberance for new experiences causes N_es to quickly drop a current project or idea and move on to something new, leaving behind a "playground" littered with uncompleted projects. In my work with groups, I have observed that during many of the experiential exercises that involve repetition—such as trying to reduce the amount of time it takes to pass a ball around a circle—the N_es get bored quickly. They are often willing to accept an intermediate level of performance improvement as "good enough" and ask to move on to something new. In fact, N_es might appear to be frittering their lives away, never completing any of their major projects and always in a state of chaos.

N_es are natural born *idea generators, par excellence*. They are ingenious creators who like to interact with their own kind in a stream-of-consciousness romp from one topic to another. To the N_e, all topics are related, making it natural to jump from one to another. During these "brainstorming" interactions, they tend to focus more on the idea than the person behind it. Anyone interacting with other N_es who is not operating in the N_e mode, might quickly become confused by the rapid jumping from topic to topic, incomplete sentences and iNtuiting understanding of what the other N_es are saying. N_es may start laughing hysterically while non-N_es looking on are left wondering what is so humorous.

The N_e's mind is constantly moving forward with little concept of time. This results in habitual tardiness, missed appointments, lost items and moving with their own chaotic agenda. One day my oldest daughter, Michele (N_e), came over with an article about how earthworms (affectionately referred to as "the girls") could improve the growth of grass in her yard. She wanted to dig for them in my yard—though it was obvious that if I had earthworms in my yard the theory was flawed. After a couple of weeks of "worming," she found a magazine article on organic fertilizer that could be made from a very specific mixture of chicken manure and water, properly cured and strained. The worms were out, "chicken manure tea" was in. Just as suddenly, she developed a strong desire to raise a puppy. Tea was out and puppies were in. And the chaos continues.

Memory. Ideas, possibilities and images generated by an N_e Type spiral into storage in symbolic memory which enables the individual to recall different images, symbols and perceptions from the past and generate new ones for the present or future. N_es are constantly generating behind-the-scenes information for inclusion in the chaotic whirlwind of symbolic memory. It is not uncommon for N_es to suffer from information overload and be unable to capture all the ideas generated. The converse is also true—thinking about doing something might cause it to be moved into memory as having actually occurred. For example, if an N_e thinks about doing something like mailing a letter or making a phone call, etc., it might be remembered as having been done.

In The Grip. The N_e's inferior function is introverted Sensing. When S_i takes control, it can cause N_es to place exaggerated attention on their bodies and begin fitness fads, exercise, diets, etc., which may result in exhaustion. Bodily sensations might be interpreted as a sign of illness—almost always an illness with dire consequences, e.g., cancer, heart problems, etc. Any one of these can lead to neurotic phobias or compulsive tendencies tied to archaic sensation. It is not uncommon to find N_es who are in the grip exaggerating physical symptoms to the point of bordering on hypochondria.

Figure 13
Extraverted iNtuiting's Character

The graphic (Figure 13) used to describe the N_e has outer space as the backdrop and an astronaut with a light bulb over his head indicating ideas. The text is flowing in a stream-of-consciousness format with numerous ideas, distractions and incomplete sentences/thoughts indicating a tendency toward boredom when the attention is focused in one area too long. The word "chaos" is dispersed across the background.

Introverted iNtuiting Types (Nᵢ): "Virtuality"

Our normal working consciousness . . . is but one special type of consciousness, whilst all about it, parted from it by the flimsiest of screens, there lie potential forms of consciousness entirely different. We may go through life without suspecting their existence; but apply the requisite stimulus, and at a touch they are all there in all their completeness.
(William James, 1890)

In contrast to the N_e, the introverted iNtuiting's world is not a constant stream of words and articulated thoughts, but rather a flow of indescribable images that, to be shared, must be converted into a verbal or visual form. When converted, these images might not make "sense" or might seem bizarre to the non-N_i. For example, when Albert Einstein related his image of flying through space in an elevator, his peers thought he was a bit strange. When someone hears Kekule's description of seeing snakes dancing and one of the snakes grabbing its tail in its mouth to form a ring, it might be difficult to understand how Kekule "discovered" the molecular structure of benzene from this image and radically changed the field of organic chemistry. Even more startling is reading the detailed account of his vision and comparing it to a description of the double helix molecular structure of DNA. Startling, because his detailed description was not of the molecular structure of benzene, but of the DNA molecule which was not known until almost 100 years later.

Mohandas Gandhi's vision for India and world peace, Dwight D. Eisenhower's images of global warfare, Thomas A. Edison's constant quest to materialize his images and James Cameron's manifestation of his images into *ET©* and *The Terminator©* movies are other examples of the powerful, unrestricted abilities of N_i and the reason the image label of *virtuality* was chosen. A virtual environment consists of an environment (world) of multi-dimensional visualizations that can be navigated and deliberately manipulated. The N_i is immersed in this type of environment and has the ability to change her point of view and interact in real time with the virtual world and the images in it. These images can be rearranged and restructured in *any* manner. *Everything is possible!* The N_i's only limitation is an inability to describe this world to others so they can have some comprehension of what is being experienced.

Table 15 shows the dominant and auxiliary N_i MBTI Types. It is interesting to note that the original proponent of the MBTI Type theory and co-author of the MBTI, Katharine C. Briggs, was an N_i. Her vision and insight were instrumental in the conceptualization of the MBTI field.

Dominant Function-Attitude	MBTI Types with N_i Dominant	MBTI Types with N_i Auxiliary
N_i	INTJ INFJ	ENTJ ENFJ

Table 15
Introverted iNtuiting MBTI Types

The introverted iNtuiting Types are oriented toward *psychic reality* and the contents of their unconscious, creating their own virtuality. Jung (1976) describes the N_i process as:

> *The perception of the images of the unconscious, produced in such inexhaustible abundance by the created energy of life, is of course fruitless from the standpoint of immediate utility. But since these images represent possible views of the world which may give life a new potential, this function, which to the outside world is the strangest of all, is as indispensable to the total psychic economy as is the corresponding human type to the psychic life of a people. Had this type not existed, there would have been no prophets in Israel.* (p. 400)

The N_i Type focuses on the subjective images created from the stimulation of the unconscious iNtuiting function by external and internal stimuli. These images are so complex and dissimilar to "objective reality" that they are difficult—sometimes impossible—for the N_i to articulate. N_i Types think, feel, see and respond to internal images. Ideas, concepts and relationships are in constant motion, changing shapes, forms and dimensions, always creating something new. Just as S_es are part of the present, N_is are *amalgamated with the future*. This gives them an uncanny ability to see the future and they often manifest as prophets, seers, artists or visionaries. Often their work is so complex or ahead of its time that it is not understood until examined by later generations. An example is the work of Jung, the depth and implications of which are just now being understood and credited.

The N_i Type not only looks and sounds different from the N_e, but is qualitatively different. The N_i thinks in images and metaphors that are difficult to articulate and only shares these thoughts once they are well developed, unlike N_es who think out loud. When a thought does escape an N_i, it might sound bizarre or inappropriate. While eating Sunday lunch with my family in a crowded restaurant and listening to my wife (Grenae, an auxiliary N_e) and two of my children (Stephen and Michele, both auxiliary N_es) discuss how actors sometimes use Preparation-H® under their eyes to draw out the wrinkles, I proffered the following thought experiment. "What if you put a lot of Preparation-H® on your hands and rubbed it all over your face except on your lips. Would it immediately draw your entire face down to your lips so that your face only had a set of lips on it?" This brought an immediate rebuke from my T_e daughter Jennifer for embarrassing the family in front of the people in the restaurant, followed closely by similar responses of shock from the other members of my family. Ideas and concepts that materialize from the unconscious may have little resemblance to the external objects or stimuli that generated their beginnings.

Behavior. The N_i tends to be quiet, distant, aloof to external reality and somewhat absent-minded. They might miss appointments or fail to notice details right under their noses. Their minds move rapidly through space with their bodies clumsily following behind. When engaged in "thought" they might walk into things, walk by a friend without speaking or generally be oblivious to the physical world around them.

The N_i's unique ability to take a complex problem, move it into their virtual world, rearrange and study it gives them an uncanny ability to simplify the complex. They do not get confused by the facts and details when solving problems. N_is love to attack the complex, but prefer to work out the solution alone. They can, however, make good team players *if* they accept the team goals and values *and* view the other team members as *competent* and *authentic*.

When N_is express themselves, their extraverted judging function (T or F) might cause them to be perceived as direct and forceful. This is often mistaken for stubbornness and inflexibility, when in reality N_is will quickly modify and adapt decisions when information is received that shows their conclusions to be incorrect. (This is not to say that they are never stubborn. INTJs, above all, can be particularly stubborn when they believe they are right—which is most of the time.) In fact, the N_i is constantly looking for a better solution to the problem even without the presence of contradictory information.

N_is are usually vague where facts are concerned such as giving directions or being able to recall the names of streets. They are not particularly good at games like Trivial Pursuit® where factual information is required about non-theoretical topics. They can become so consumed by their work or play (the distinction between work and play being whether they enjoy it or not) that they lose track of time and might neglect their physical needs, failing to get enough rest, sleep or proper nutrition.

Memory. N_i is constantly feeding images, ideas and thoughts into the symbolic memory as well as retrieving data from it for use on current thoughts. Unfortunately, much of the steady stream of images going into symbolic memory does not make it into permanent storage or into a retrievable area. Consequently, many of the N_i's best *images* are lost. Another problem with N_i's contribution to memory is that the data may be of such an abstract form that it has to be modified to be retrieved, resulting in a loss of meaning. This may lead to the memory of an event not coinciding with objective reality.

In the Grip. The N_i's inferior function, extraverted Sensing (S_e), tends to be very intense when it is allowed to break through into consciousness. While in the grip, the N_i might make more factual mistakes than normal, which generates even more stress. They can become obsessed with facts to the point of becoming overwhelmed, almost paralyzed by them. Sensory experiences take control of the normally "in control" individual. When in the grip, they might be easily angered and show it by uncommon outbursts of hostility. Their long-range, future focus and multiple-options approach become severely truncated. They tend to make lists of everything in an attempt to get control of something.

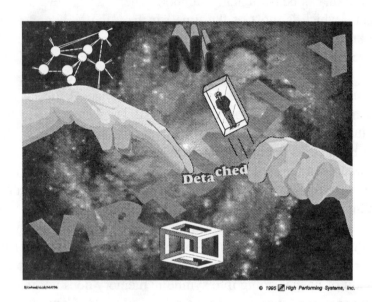

Figure 14
Introverted iNtuiting's Character

The graphic (Figure 14) chosen to represent the N_i has the cosmos as a background, representing the "far out" where anything is possible and the deepest thoughts occur. The graphic is filled with mostly three-dimensional images, not words per se. The images include Einstein's elevator traveling through space, illusive forms and a vortex. A set of hands manipulating images provides the metaphorical suggestion of the interaction between the N_i and this domain. The word "virtuality" sprawls across the cosmos.

Summary

Table 16 shows the estimated distribution of the perceiving function-attitude Types (dominant) in the U. S. population. The contrast of percentages between S_i and N_i is striking.

S_e	N_e
10 %	11 %
S_i	N_i
27 %	6 %

Table 16
Perceiving Function-Attitude Percentages[29]

The perceiving function-attitudes provide more than just a means of perceiving the external and internal worlds. They define the world and its boundaries in which we *allow* ourselves to exist. A world of sensuosity and surreal experiences, of chaos and virtuality. To be functional, our world must be structured and organized and have defining values. The creation of these attributes requires use of the judging function-attitudes.

---

[29] The percentages presented here are based on the CPP data.

The Judging Function-Attitudes

A judgment that is truly rational will appeal to the objective and the subjective factor equally and do justice to both. But that would be an ideal case and would presuppose an equal development of both extraversion and introversion. In practice, however, either movement excludes the other, and, so long as this dilemma remains, they cannot exist side by side but at best successively. (Jung, 1976a, pp. 391-392)

Judging Function-Attitudes

The judging functions (T & F) combine with the attitudes (E & I) to form four judging function-attitude Types, extraverted Thinking (T_e), introverted Thinking (T_i), extraverted Feeling (F_e) and introverted Feeling (F_i), as shown in Figure 15.

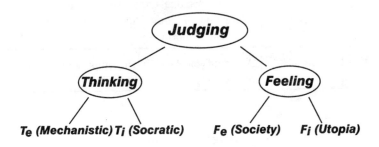

Figure 15
Judging Function-Attitudes

An interesting sidebar is that when Jung began to study the judging functions, he did not separate them into both extraverted and introverted function Types. Instead, he viewed Thinking as having only an introverted attitude and Feeling as having only an extraverted attitude. After a *"more thorough investigation of the material,"* Jung (1976a) came to the conclusion that the judging functions were associated with both attitudes.

The image labels for the judging function-attitude Types are *"mechanistic," "socratic," "society"* and *"utopia."* An abstract definition of each label is given in Table 17.

F-A	Image	Abstraction
T_e	Mechanistic	Orderly, logical and mechanically structured thought process and behavior.
T_i	Socratic	A philosophical quest for the rational truth through the use of penetrating, systematic questioning and doubt.
F_e	Society	Friendly, personal and organized pattern of interaction with others in accordance with established "norms."
F_i	Utopia	A cognitive "place" having impossibly ideal relationships and social schemes.

Table 17
Image Definitions

Extraverted Thinking Types (T_e): "Mechanistic"

In 1687 Newton published the Philosophie Naturalis Principia Mathematicia [*Mathematical Principles of Natural Philosophy*]. . . . *He explained how a single mathematical law could account for phenomenon that occurred in the heavens, the tides and the motions of objects on the earth. Newton painted the universe as a large clockwork machine in which everything had a cause and produced an effect, a deterministic universe based on continuous motion.* (Thompson, 1996)

Sir Isaac Newton appeared to have organized the universe with one mathematical principle that has been used for everything from space travel to designing business organizations. T_es are driven to logically organize the external world around them and prescribe defining principles of cause and effect. They create a *mechanistic* world of orderly, logical and structured processes. Charles Darwin (1859), in *The Origin of the Species,* applied T_e in such a convincing manner that his theory has been accepted as fact, and mounting evidence against it continues to be suppressed. (This might occur because there are so many T_es in academic positions of authority who have a need for a guiding principle like the one Darwin proposed.)

From a Myers-Briggs perspective the T_e is represented by ESTJ and ENTJ in the dominant extraverted form and ISTJ and INTJ in the auxiliary form. Dominant T_es aggressively attempt to organize the external world and those around them. The auxiliary T_es are also busily organizing the external world but might not share that structure with others unless asked.

Dominant Function-Attitude	MBTI Types with Dominant T_e	MBTI Types with Auxiliary T_e
T_e	ESTJ ENTJ	ISTJ INTJ

Table 18
Extraverted Thinking MBTI Types

As an extraverted process, T_e revolves around the external world and, although it is an intellectual process, is not necessarily connected to intelligence or quality of thought. It has extensity rather than intensity as its aim and, as such, can be influenced by external experience and societal norms. According to Jung (1976a), Thinking presupposes a judgment.

> *This type will, by definition, be a man whose constant endeavour—in so far, of course, as he is a pure type—is to make all his activities dependent on intellectual conclusions, which in the last resort*

*are always oriented by objective data, whether
these be external facts or generally accepted ideas.
This type of man elevates objective reality, or an
objectively oriented intellectual formula, into the
ruling principle not only for himself, but his whole
environment.* (Jung, 1976a, pp. 346-347)

T_es establish a mechanistic order of the environment,
objectify emotional situations and ascribe meaning to external
data. The T_e operates by a dynamic, formula-driven system of
rules, ideals and principles (Sharp, 1987) which aim at producing
a more consistent understanding of the universe and constancy of
relationships (Newman, 1990). T_es continually strive to define a
mechanistic perfection as demonstrated by Newton and Darwin.

Behavior. The T_e behaves mechanistically and is cause-
and-effect driven—if this button is pushed then this happens.
Their system of ruling principles and impersonal judgment causes
them to take a definite stand on everything. Unlike F_es, in the T_e's
world all situations are *black* and *white; there are no shades of
gray,* and the emphasis is always on the external world rather than
the internal. When their actions are questioned they *always* have
a "logical" reason (in their minds) for what they do and are quick
to provide the rationale, in detail, when challenged. F_es often
respond to the T_e's response when challenged with, "Don't take it
so personally." T_es, in most cases, are not taking it personally.
Unlike the F_es, they are reacting to the lack of logic by the person
disagreeing with them. I once heard a T_e say, "I'm not taking it
personally, it's just that what you are saying doesn't make sense
logically!"

Everything that agrees with the T_e's ruling principle is
right; everything that disagrees with it is wrong. T_es want to be
able to live their lives according to a universal law and to have
everyone and everything follow the same ruling principle. They
judge themselves and others by "shoulds" and "oughts" and try to

convince others to see things the same way they see them.

T_es are driven by the structuring quality of Thinking to *plan*, *organize* and *make decisions* about everything around them—their personal, work and home lives. They have a high need for closure and forward movement. They do not like to revisit "closed" issues. Their interactions might seem aggressive, blunt and "right." Even though they do not give the outward appearance of having strong feelings or emotional ties with others, they can be the most faithful of all friends.

Memory. Intellectual memory manifests as a result of the Thinking function. T_e's contribution to intellectual memory is the construction of a library or relational database of intellectual knowledge, principles and rules as well as the provision of meaning, logic and organization of external data gathered by perception. This includes the development of objective organizational taxonomies for structuring the outer world. The T_e portion of intellectual memory interacts with S_e and N_e during the act of perception in such a manner as to influence, both quantitatively and qualitatively, what is actually perceived (Newman, 1990).

In The Grip. When the T_e's inferior function, introverted Feeling (F_i), takes control, the black and white judgments become "love or hate." Rilke's (1984) phrase *"I love you but it is none of your business"* takes on a special meaning for the T_e and is reflected in an invisible faithfulness that can last forever. Their behavior can become childish and fanatical. A T_e might spend a lifetime settling problems, reorganizing firms or starting things, and only at the end of life begin to ask mournfully, "What was the purpose of my life?" At such a moment, the inferior function, F_i, takes control (von Franz & Hillman, 1971). The T_e begins to question his or her own self-worth, takes criticism very personally or expresses uncontrolled emotions.

Mystical feelings attached to the T_e's ideals come under the influence of F_i and might result in impersonal, cold, unfriendly or selfish behavior. The T_e might neglect his family's interests or engage in petty, aggressive or mistrustful behavior. An air of righteousness might appear.

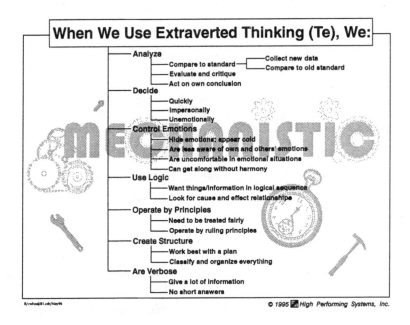

Figure 16
Extraverted Thinking's Character

The graphic (Figure 16) that represents extraverted Thinking is black and white to indicate "either/or" judgment and has the text organized and structured into information domains. The large amount of text represents a vast collection of information and long answers to questions. The clock and gears represent the mechanistic nature of the T_e process. The tools add to the impersonal approach. The word "mechanistic" is aligned across the background.

Introverted Thinking Types (T$_i$): "Socratic"

> *I want to know what is characteristic of piety*
> *which makes all actions pious . . . that I may have*
> *it to turn to, and to use as a standard whereby to*
> *judge your actions and those of other men.*
> (Socrates, 400 B.C.[30])

Socrates was searching for a ruling principle or an algorithm with which he could judge thoughts and actions as pious or non-pious. He was on a philosophical quest for the *rational truth* through the use of penetrating, systematic questioning and doubt. Together with his students, such as Plato and Plato's student Aristotle, Socrates' T$_i$ had a major influence on much of western thought and culture (Russell & Norvig, 1995).

Rene Descartes is probably most widely known for locking himself in a room for two weeks during a snowstorm and formulating his famous statement, "*I think, therefore I am.*" When he said "I am" he was referring to *being* and "I think" referred to *change*. This was the beginning of an attempt to construct a

---

[30] Hubert Dreyfus, 1979.

complete theory of the Universe using *being* and *change* as its foundation. Descartes was one of the first to use logical thought in physical science, a technique that was later used by Newton (Thompson, 1996).

The T_i lives in the *Socratic* world with Kant, Nietzche and Linus (from the *Peanuts*© comic strip) where the objective of life is the constant seeking and questioning of truth and its ruling principles.

The dominant T_i is represented in Myers-Briggs terminology by the ISTP and the INTP (Table 19). The auxiliary T_is are ESTP (dominant S_e) and ENTP (dominant N_e). Although a person's language and surface behavior tend to be indicative of the extraverted function, the long-term "driver" of the personality is the dominant function, even when it is introverted. When the dominant function is extraverted such as with an ENTP, the influence of the introverted auxiliary function will be evident.

Dominant Function-Attitude	MBTI Types with T_i Dominant	MBTI Types with T_i Auxiliary
T_i	ISTP INTP	ESTP ENTP

Table 19
Introverted Thinking MBTI Types

With an introverted attitude, the T_i's energy flow is inward to the internal world and results in everything becoming thought. The T_i operates with intensity, not extensity. Although introverted, this Type can be strongly influenced by external *ideas*. The T_i is constantly concerned with ordering ideas rather than objects and clarifying ideas *before* dealing with external data. They begin problem solving from the internal world and work outward to the external world then back to the internal world. What is most important to the T_i is new views, not new facts (Meier, 1995). Jung (1976a) believed that facts were of secondary importance to the T_i—most important was the subjective idea. The T_i is proficient at making conceptual connections between disparate ideas (Singer, 1994). They use a positive, synthetic (combining ideas/views into new ones) Thinking process. The more contact they have with the object, the more *mythological* they become. Jung (1976a) states that this Type *"evaporates into a representation of the irrepresentable, far beyond anything that could be expressed in an image"* (p. 382).

Behavior. The behavior of the T_i Type might appear cold, inflexible, arbitrary or reclusive. Jung (1976a) states that the T_i

> *will shrink from no danger in building this world of ideas, and never shrinks when thinking a thought because it might prove to be dangerous, subversive, heretical or wounding to other people's feelings, he is nonetheless beset by the greatest anxiety if ever he has to make it an objective reality. . . . if in his eyes his product appears correct and true then it must be so in practice and others have got to bow to its truth. Hardly ever will he go out of his way to win anyone's appreciation of it, especially anyone of influence.* (p. 384)

T_is tend to be stubborn, headstrong and difficult to influence and, at times, fail to comprehend the importance of their relationships to people or things because these are of secondary importance to them. This makes the T_i unconscious of or blind to other people. Living in an inner world, T_is might fail to realize how others see them. T_is tend to think that everyone sees the illusion the T_is have created in their own minds, instead of reality.

I worked with a T_i colleague who, although very intelligent, often engaged in questionable ethical behaviors as if he were invisible to those around him. Once he even made the statement to the work group, "*I will be in the office tomorrow, but you won't see me.*" (Unfortunately the group did see him.)

Getting T_is to admit that what is clear to them might not be so clear to others can be a difficult task. T_is might throw themselves at people who do not understand, which could cause them to think that *people are basically stupid.* Jung (1976a) states that they often come across as inconsiderate, prickly, arrogant, sour and anti-social. At times they confuse their ideas (internal "truths") with external reality, then defend their ideas voraciously. When confronted with problems, they prefer to withdraw to work them out. The T_i Type can be difficult to understand, to say the least. At times, they may try to placate people just to prevent them from becoming a nuisance. Others observing this might see the T_i as having an ulterior motive. The relentless pursuit and critique of knowledge by Kant and Nietzsche are characteristic of T_i.

The T_i's logic can be seen in the following example. One Saturday as my family was leaving the house, I observed an umbrella (collapsed and fastened) leaning against the door frame and realized it belonged to one of our neighbors. When I asked, "Who used the Smiths' umbrella?" all three children said they had not used it. Still not convinced, I asked my T_i son, Stephen (eight years old at the time), "Did you carry the Smiths' umbrella to our house?" He said, "Yes." "Why didn't you tell me that the first time?" I asked. He replied, "You asked me if I used it. I didn't *use* it, I just *carried* it." You will often hear the precision of the T_i function-attitude come out in anyone's language.

Memory. The role of introverted Thinking in memory is in ordering, structuring and evaluating ideas to be stored for later comparison to new data. Precise taxonomies are created for storage and retrieval, even if it means forcing data to fit—or rejecting the data altogether!

In The Grip. When the inferior function of extraverted Feeling (F_e) takes control, the T_i's feelings can be easily poisoned by others and take on a love or hate relationship. The phrase "*I love you, and it will be your business; I'll make it your business!*" (von Franz & Hillman, 1971) holds true while the inferior is in control. Their feelings flow toward the external world and can become whimsical.

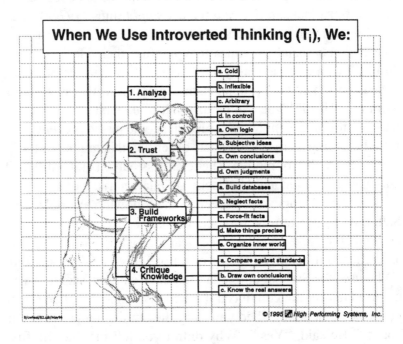

Figure 17
Introverted Thinking's Character

When using the inferior function, T_is are extremely vulnerable and can be easily influenced and exploited by others. The T_i Type tends to pick people as friends who turn out to be either very "good" or very "bad" friends. They may become sensitive to criticism or unable to express their emotions and feel like they are victims of a lack of appreciation or friendship. The T_i Type also has a tendency to have a vague fear of the opposite sex when the inferior is in control (Jung, 1976a).

The T_i graphic (Figure 17) is similar to the one representing T_e in that it is also black and white. It is, however, much more structured and rigid and the categorical taxonomies are more precise—hence the grid system. The graphic in the background is reminiscent of Rodin's sculpture "The Thinker," and the word "Socratic" is aligned across the top.

Extraverted Feeling Types (F$_e$): "Society"

> *A painting, for instance, is called "beautiful"*
> *because a painting hung in a drawing room and*
> *bearing a well-known signature is generally*
> *assumed to be beautiful, or because to call it*
> *"hideous" would presumably offend the family or*
> *its fortunate possessor, or because the visitor*
> *wants to create a pleasant feeling atmosphere, for*
> *which purpose everything must be felt as*
> *agreeable.* (Jung, 1976a, p. 355)

The F$_e$ lives in *society*, a world of interpersonal interactions governed by organized patterns of relationships that are supposed to be characterized by polite, courteous and considerate behaviors. These common traditions have global rules for "appropriate" behavior during collective activities. For example, psychological literature shows that the emotions shown on the four "faces" above can be identified by a five-year-old child in any country. They have learned from society the meaning of such expressions. In his book *The Expression of Emotion in Man and Animals*, Charles Darwin (1872) demonstrated that even animals recognize the appropriateness of certain "societal" behaviors. The F$_e$ is the *gatekeeper* for the societal norms—rightness and wrongness—by which human societies are supposed to live.

Former president George Bush was nicknamed "Have-half" as a child, connoting his propensity for sharing whatever he had with others (Keirsey & Choiniere, 1992). Later, during the Gulf War as the NATO forces were moving rapidly toward Baghdad, he called a humanitarian halt to the massive destruction of enemy lives rather than continue the slaughter. This turned out to be one of the most criticized actions of his presidency. He also made numerous references to his quests to create a "new world order" and to recreate family values in America. His F_e behavior and resulting focus on improving society have been observable throughout his life.

Dominant Function-Attitude	MBTI Types with F_e Dominant	MBTI Types with F_e Auxiliary
F_e	ESFJ ENFJ	ISFJ INFJ

Table 20
Extraverted Feeling MBTI Types

Extraverted Feeling (F_e) is strongly influenced by changes in the F_e's environment over time. The more focused on an object in the external world F_es become, the more impersonal their feelings toward it. F_es constantly evaluate external objects under the strong influence of societal norms. A slight change in the situation can dramatically change their behavior. The F_e can appear moody or might experience manic depressive periods. I once had an F_e office manager who could suddenly change from warm, friendly and charming to pouty, angry and aggressive if I came into the office in an N_i mode ("off in the cosmos") and didn't say "good morning" (a "must do" behavior in the normative society). My perceived bad mood "caused" her to be in a bad mood, and she then convinced herself that it was going to be a bad day.

> *People of this type have at times the most negative and depreciatory thoughts about the very persons most valued by their feelings. Indeed, the presence of such thinking, normally dormant in the background, is one of the main indicators that extraverted feeling is the dominant function.* (Sharp, 1987, p. 53)

Behavior. Extraverted Feeling Types tend to personify the "people person." Described by Hillman (von Franz & Hillman, 1971) as the *charming feeler*, the F_e is outgoing, friendly and focused on relationships. The F_e may at times show *"extravagant displays of feeling, gushing talk, love, expostulations, etc., which ring hollow: 'The lady doth protest too much'"* (Jung, 1976a). This Type "knows" the appropriate behaviors for all situations and readily makes judgments (valuations) that are fitting for the situation. F_es know what they like and what they dislike and how to put others' needs above their own. They are able to feel others' situations and, consequently, say the appropriate thing to make others feel good or important. Because personal relationships are so valuable to F_es, they tend to make friends easily and have an abundance of friends for whom they will sacrifice themselves if necessary. They tend to roll along through society with few illusions about people, spread an attitude of acceptance and are always "jumping into the breach" for other people (von Franz & Hillman, 1971).

F_es do not have to think about what someone or something is worth to them, they just *know* (Sharp, 1987). To the extraverted Feeling Type, *what cannot be felt cannot be thought.*

The F$_e$ personality

appears adjusted in relation to external conditions. Her feelings harmonize with objective situations and general values. This is seen nowhere more clearly than in her love choice: the "suitable" man is loved, and no one else; he is suitable not because he appeals to her hidden subjective nature—about which he usually knows nothing—but because he comes up to all the reasonable expectations in the matter of age, position, income, size and respectability of his family, etc. (Jung, 1976a, p. 356)

Memory. F$_e$ serves as an *assimilation* process for building affective memories of *personal relationships, values* and *emotions* over time. That is, F$_e$ absorbs information into memory, changing memory to make it similar to the event taking place. Memory is altered to reflect the current situation—*an act of adjustment to external criteria* (Sharp, 1987). This may account for the numerous mood swings and the strong influence of the external world. F$_e$ memory is dynamic, constantly changing, vacillating and producing *shades of gray*. Emotional energy is built up as is sensitivity to issues, which may result in the F$_e$ having a "short fuse."

F$_e$ memory, which can be easily articulated, is public domain. "Feelings" are not only shared with the present, they become the present. Although an F$_e$'s feelings can change quickly, if you want to know how an F$_e$ feels about something in the present, just listen. Affective memory is also closely related to the person's values (von Franz & Hillman, 1971).

In The Grip. When the F$_e$'s inferior function, introverted Thinking (T$_i$), takes over, the F$_e$ can be "the coldest person on earth." Under stress they become theatrical, mechanical and calculating (von Franz & Hillman, 1971). Their behavior manifests as faulty "nothing-but" or "either-or" thinking and tends to devalue their most valued objects. When this happens, the F_e's behavior might become infantile, archaic or negative and be easily influenced by what they hear or see. They lose the ability to think independently and could become *"sterile, spiteful and hurtful"* (Meier, 1995). While in the grip they can be extremely self-critical.

In order to avoid this type of behavior, F_es might try to surround themselves with people continuously. This helps prevent T_i from entering into consciousness and questioning the person's very existence.

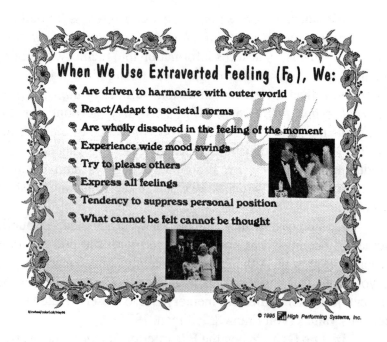

Figure 18
Extraverted Feeling's Character

The F_e graphic has a gradational yellow background surrounded by flowers, indicating a gradual coloring of the F_e's valuation of people, events and things. Because people are not graphics or images to the F_e, the people on the graphic are real family photos. One picture contains an extended family (three generations); the wedding picture exemplifies the tradition of marriage and one of the protocols of the marriage event—the bride and groom feeding each other wedding cake. Families, couples, children and social institutions in general play a major role in the life and psyche of the F_e. The word "Society" is displayed across the back of the graphic.

Introverted Feeling Types (F$_i$): "Utopia"

What Is To Be Desired?
Self-respect—to be part of the solution, not part
of the problem

Love—to love the human beings that mean the
most to me [be a help and comfort to them when
and if they need it] & contribute to their lives if
I can

Peace of Mind—to avoid mistakes that make me
regret the past or fear the future

Involvement—always   to   be   tremendously
interested

Understanding—to be able to incorporate the
things [&] people & ideas that happen to me in a
coherent concept of the world

Freedom—to work at what interests me most

Isabel B. Myers[31]

---

[31] Saunders, 1991, p. 183.

The quotation above by Isabel B. Myers was found among her papers shortly after her death in 1980. The handwritten page described her personal philosophy of life by which she tried to live. It is indicative of the F_i who has made significant progress on the journey of individuation.

The introverted Feeling Type lives in Cinderella's castle in the middle of an idealistic, *utopian* Garden of Eden shut off to the outer world by a thorn-covered wall. Inside the wall everyone and everything behaves the way they "should." My wife, Grenae (F_i), summed up what I have heard many F_is voice when she said, "Reality is harsh and should be avoided if at all possible."

Dominant Function-Attitude	MBTI Types with F_i Dominant	MBTI Types with F_i Auxiliary
F_i	ISFP INFP	ESFP ENFP

Table 21
Introverted Feeling MBTI Types

Introverted Feeling Types are personified by Rilke's (1984) phrase *"I love you, but it is none of your business."* They are the most difficult of all the Types to understand because they allow so little of themselves to appear on the surface, and the wall surrounding them is almost impossible to scale. Jung (1976a) used the phrase "Still waters run deep" when describing this Type because *"Their depth of feeling can only be guessed."* Hillman described them as the "deep feelers" (1971).

The F_i process is such that everything is *felt*, and internal images manifest as *values*. F_is are driven to judge people, things and thoughts by their *own* internal values and do not readily change their values to conform with those of society. F_is will only submit to peer pressure *if* their peers' actions are in accordance with the F_i's own beliefs (Singer, 1994).

Behavior. The F_i may appear to have no feelings and can be negative or profoundly indifferent to people. They tend to shy away from parties, etc., because they gather too much data (they have an extraverted perceiving function) to be evaluated. When F_is are members of a group they tend to be the *ethical backbone*, influencing the group by their behavior alone. F_is believe they understand everyone else very well, but often perceive themselves as being misunderstood by others. The positive feelings of F_is must be inferred indirectly because their outward demeanor is typically harmonious and inconspicuous and does not necessarily indicate their inner feelings.

Jung (1976a) says that the F_i shows *"little effort to respond to the real emotions of the other person."* Strangers are shown no special attention. The easiest place to see F_is express their feelings is with their children. Even though F_is are Feeling Types, they are different from F_es in that they do not seem to enjoy the interpersonal closeness of a "group hug" with strangers. F_es, on the other hand, seem to enjoy a good hug with almost anyone.

F_is can be mistaken for Thinking Types because of their perceived lack of "warmth and friendliness." Their outward appearance might seem cold at times.

> *Although there is a constant readiness for peaceful and harmonious co-existence, strangers are shown no touch of amicability, no gleam of responsive warmth, but are met with apparent indifference or repelling coldness. Often they are made to feel entirely superfluous. Faced with anything that might carry her away or arouse enthusiasm, this type observes a benevolent though critical neutrality, coupled with a faint trace of superiority that soon takes the wind out of the sails of the*

> *sensitive person. Any stormy emotion, however,*
> *will be struck down with murderous coldness,*
> *unless it happens to catch the woman on the*
> *unconscious side—that is, unless it hits her*
> *feelings by arousing a primordial image. In that*
> *case, she simply feels paralyzed for the moment,*
> *and this in due course and invariably produces an*
> *even more obstinate resistance that will hit the*
> *other person at his most vulnerable spot.* (Jung,
> 1976a, p. 389)

Memory. The F_i portion of affective memory operates at a much deeper level than F_e and uses an *accommodating* principle of processing data. That is, rather than affective memory being readily changed by incoming data, as with the F_e's assimilating process, the data are actually changed (accommodated) to fit the existing memory and values. This might account for the F_i's relatively stable values and resistance to peer pressure. Data inconsistent with the F_i's values are resisted, causing change to occur slowly. Stored memories tend to be in a kinesthetic form which is very difficult to articulate. F_i memories are subjective, private and idealistic and are attached to the person's core values.

In The Grip. When the inferior function of T_e takes control, F_is might seem distant. *"With the thinking function in charge they may go racing with a few ideas through a tremendous amount of material"* (von Franz & Hillman, 1971, p. 61). They become interested in and can get lost in an immense number of facts and paralyzed by the compulsive ordering of things. If the ego is unchecked, it may result in vanity, bossiness or similar types of behavior.

> *The egocentrized subject now comes to feel the*
> *power and importance of the devalued object. She*
> *begins consciously to feel "what other people*

think." Naturally, other people are thinking all
sorts of mean things, scheming evil, contriving
plots, secret intrigues, etc. In order to forestall
them, she herself is obliged to start counter-
intrigues, to suspect others and sound them out,
and weave counterplots. Beset by rumours, she
must make frantic efforts to get her own back and
be top dog. Endless clandestine rivalries spring up,
and in these embittered struggles she will shrink
from no baseness or meanness, and will even
prostitute her virtues in order to play the trump
card. Such a state of affairs must end in
exhaustion. (Jung, 1976a, p. 391)

The F_i might become destructive, directing venomous criticism at other people and the world in general (Meier, 1995), or be seen as tyrannical, stiff and unyielding (von Franz & Hillman, 1971). They begin to question their own competence and self-worth, and apply faulty logic to the motives of others.

The graphic (Figure 19) for F_i has a yellow background (darker that the F_e graphic) and depicts a utopian world contained inside a high wall with thorns growing along the top. A magnifying glass is used to aid in seeing what is deep inside the F_i's walls. Beautiful plants, waterfalls, streams and various types of small birds and animals inhabit the garden. The family members, dressed in simple togas and sandals, are always together. It is a beautiful, peaceful place. The word "utopia" is written across the background.

Figure 19
Introverted Feeling's Character

Summary

The judging function-attitudes provide more than just a means of judging the objective and the subjective perceptions of our world. They provide the intellectual meaning, structure, valuation and emotional and personal parameters attached to each perception. Our perceptual world now becomes a mechanistic, Socratically-defined society placed in juxtaposition with a utopian ideal.

Table 22 shows the approximate percentage of each of the judging function-attitudes in the United States population.

T_e	F_e
13 %	12 %
T_i	F_i
12 %	9 %

Table 22
Judging Function-Attitudes Distribution[32]

---

[32] The percentages presented here are based on CPP data.

Concluding Remarks

Every individual is an exception to the rule. Hence one can never give a description of a type, no matter how complete, that would apply to more than one individual, despite the fact that in some ways it aptly characterizes thousands of others. Conformity is one side of man, uniqueness is the other. (Jung, 1976a, p. 516)

Type Development

Sixteen combinations of function-attitudes are shown in Chapter 1, Table 1. These represent Jung's psychological Types. The Myers-Briggs Type codes for these Types are shown in Table 4. Although only two functions are shown in each Type code, each of the Types possesses all eight function-attitudes. Both Jungian and Myers-Briggs Type development theories prescribe, either directly or indirectly, a sequence of differentiation of the four functions—dominant, auxiliary, tertiary then inferior.

A review of the literature reveals two interesting facts. First, it shows consistency in the assignment of attitudes to the dominant, auxiliary and inferior functions and disagreement over the attitude of the tertiary function. Three basic positions emerge as to the attitude of the tertiary function: (1) it is opposite the auxiliary; (2) it is the same as the auxiliary; (3) it can be either the same or opposite. Although Jung vacillates on this issue, he leans toward the first position.

The second interesting fact is that treatment of the developmental sequence in the Type literature seems to stop with the four basic function-attitudes assigned to each Type. For example, according to position 1 above, an ENTP has a developmental sequence of $N_e T_i F_e S_i$. With the exception of the attitude of the tertiary function (F), well-known Jungians and Type practitioners tend to agree with this sequence. Since each psychological Type has all eight function-attitudes, where are the other four and where are they in the developmental sequence?

Beebe's Model

Dr. John Beebe, a Jungian analyst, proposes an answer to this question with his *personality schema* of Type development (Beebe, 1996). Beebe has used his research, studies and observations from his therapy practice over the years to develop a model in which the archetypal complexes carry the eight function-attitudes. Beebe begins by defining the dominant-inferior polar opposites as the *spine* of the personality (Figure 20[33]). The spine configuration places the dominant function at the top of a vertical axis (nearest the head in the metaphor and the most conscious) and the inferior at the bottom (nearest the feet and the farthest from consciousness). Rotating the spine 180° forms the opposite personality spine, accounting for all eight combinations.

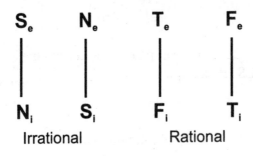

Figure 20
Beebe's Spines

Whichever attitude the dominant function takes, the inferior takes the opposite. For example, if the dominant function is extraverted, the inferior function is introverted.

The auxiliary and tertiary functions form a horizontal axis that Beebe refers to as *arms* with the auxiliary function on the left when looking at the model (Figure 21). The auxiliary function has the opposite attitude of the dominant function and the tertiary has the same as the dominant. Each of the arms in Figure 21 can be rotated 180° to form its opposite combination.

---

[33] For the purpose of consistency I have modified Beebe's nomenclature by converting his function-attitude codes to the ones used in this book. For example, in his models he uses capital letters with the attitude first, such as ES to represent extraverted Sensing.

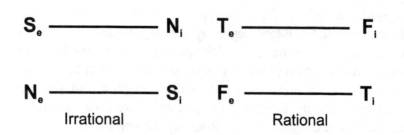

Figure 21
Beebe's Arms

Figure 22 shows the spine and arm combination and Figure 23 gives an ESTP example.

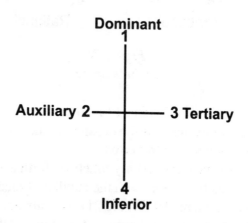

Figure 22
Spine and Arm Combination

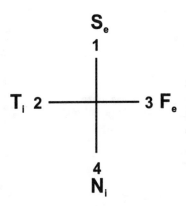

Figure 23
ESTP Example

The other half of Beebe's model consists of the second set of four function-attitudes. These are arranged in the same sequence as the first four; that is, the opposite attitude of the dominant is at the top, the opposite attitude of the inferior is at the bottom, etc. Figure 24 shows the second set of four function-attitudes in relation to the first four function-attitudes using an ESTP as an example.

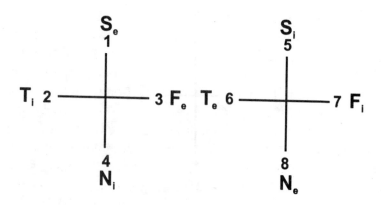

Figure 24
The Relationship of the Eight Function-Attitudes of an ESTP

You will note that the eight function-attitude positions have numbers assigned to them. The first four numbers were selected to be consistent with classical Jungian theory, i.e., dominant is 1, auxiliary is 2, tertiary is 3 and inferior is 4. Positions five through eight *"simply match the first four so there won't be too much confusion. The numbering is highly arbitrary and not intended to imply a developmental sequence"* (Beebe, 1996).

At this point in the development of his model, Beebe[34] is relatively confident that "normal" Type development (if there is such a thing) proceeds in the sequence of 1, 2, 3, 7, 4 and then maybe 5, 8 and 6, although the last three in the sequence are highly speculative at this time. His rationale for going to position 7 before 4 is that he has seen evidence that one must deal with the *shadow* of the 3rd function (i.e., position 7) before being able to individuate the 4th function.

---

[34]   See Anne Singer Harris (1996), *Living with Paradox: An Introduction to Jungian Psychology*, Brooks/Cole Publishing Company, Chapters 4-5 for a more detailed treatment of Beebe's model.

For example, according to Beebe's model, an ESTP's function-attitudes would normally be expected to develop in the sequence of (1) S_e, (2) T_i, (3) F_e, (7) F_i, (4) N_i, (5) S_i, (8) N_e & (6) T_e. Beebe also suggests that Type development is complex, with numerous external factors such as strong parental or environmental influence having an impact on not only the sequence, but the extent of Type development. An example of a maladaptive development is when a person does not develop the auxiliary second, but rather develops the tertiary. Developing the tertiary second results in the pairing of two functions with the same attitude. For example, S_e and F_e for an ESTP—an "unbalanced" combination. Development of the tertiary second tends to be more prominent in women and minority groups because they are encouraged to behave more "childlike" (Harris, 1996).

Marshall's Model

Dr. Allen Marshall has proposed a developmental sequence similar to Beebe's. Marshall (1996) agrees with Beebe's spine and arm placement of the eight function-attitudes but sees the two attitude components of a function, e.g., extraverted Sensing and introverted Sensing, as being *linked* together. When an ESTP differentiates S_e, for example, it has to be separated from S_i, thereby leaving S_i also differentiated. Figure 25 shows a three-dimensional representation of how Marshall's model might look with the attitudes linked and following a complete function differentiation sequence.

According to this model, an ESTP's expected function-attitude developmental sequence would be S_e, S_i, T_i, T_e, F_e, F_i, N_i, N_e.

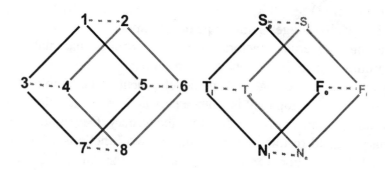

Figure 25
Marshall's Linked Functional Differentiation Model

Spoto's Model

Angelo Spoto, a prominent Jungian analyst, proposes a more radical approach to Type development. Spoto (1995) suggests that the function-attitudes tend to develop through one of three processes that he describes as *simple, complex* and *aberrant*[35]. In the simple process, only one function-attitude becomes differentiated (Figure 26), and this normally occurs during the first half of life. For example, a simple Type ENTJ might only differentiate T_e and fail to differentiate an auxiliary; or an INTJ might only differentiate N_i.

When observing or listening to a simple Type, the differentiated function-attitude stands out so strongly that the person almost seems one-sided—not to be confused with an initial

---

[35] For a more detailed treatment of Spoto's "Types," see chapter 6 in his book, *Jung's Typology in Perspective*, Chiron Publications, Revised Edition, 1995.

conversation with an introvert. When using the MBTI, it is not unusual for individuals to have a high preference score[36] for one function and be "borderline" on the others. This might be indicative of a simple Type.

$$S_e \qquad S_i \qquad N_e \qquad N_i$$

$$T_e \qquad T_i \qquad F_e \qquad F_i$$

Figure 26
Spoto's Simple Types

The complex Types include a balance of the attitudes and of the irrational and rational functions through the differentiation of both a dominant and auxiliary function-attitude (Figure 27). The development of the complex Type fits more closely with the Jungian and Myers-Briggs concepts of Type development and tends to be the most common, *if* preference scores on the MBTI are an indication.

$$S_e T_i \qquad S_i T_e \qquad T_e S_i \qquad T_i S_e$$

$$S_e F_i \qquad S_i F_e \qquad T_e N_i \qquad T_i N_e$$

$$N_e T_i \qquad N_i T_e \qquad F_e S_i \qquad F_i S_e$$

$$N_e F_i \qquad N_i F_e \qquad F_e N_i \qquad F_i N_e$$

Figure 27
Spoto's Complex Types

---

[36] Preference scores on the MBTI are not necessarily indicative of function differentiation, but it would be interesting to explore the relationship between preference scores and Spoto's Types.

For Jung, the "problem of opposites" during the first half of life was focused on the irrational and rational functions vying for the auxiliary position and not a battle between the dominant and inferior functions (Spoto, 1995).

Spoto's third Type is labeled aberrant (or "unstable") because these do not follow the expected or predicted combinations of attitudes and functions—nothing pathological is implied. Figure 28 shows examples of these aberrant Types. You will note that aberrant Types include the combination of two introverted or two extraverted functions and/or the combination of two irrational or rational functions. Spoto believes that in most cases Type will develop along either the simple or complex route. He further elaborates:

> *I respect the ego's need to maintain its balance and autonomy, especially in the first half of life, but do not want to make balance and autonomy an absolute for all individuals in all circumstances.* (p. 162)

Spoto lists three possible advantages to the aberrant Type: (1) they may have a greater tolerance for ambiguity, (2) they may have less need to control their outer or inner lives and (3) they may be more creative.

$S_e N_e$	$T_e F_e$	$S_e S_i$	$S_i T_i$
$S_i N_i$	$T_i F_i$	$N_e N_i$	$S_i F_i$
$N_e S_e$	$F_e T_e$	$T_e T_i$	$N_i T_i$
$N_i S_i$	$F_i T_i$	$F_e F_i$	$N_i F_i$

Figure 28
Spoto's Aberrant Types
(Partial Listing)

Spoto's model of Type development allows for a much greater degree of flexibility of development and environmental influences than other theories and also lends support to Beebe's "unbalanced" Type development. My experience with Type development tends to support Spoto's model.

Type Dynamics

Mathematically, linearity implies that a system is the sum of its parts. This mathematical description also imputes a uni-directionality. That is, the cause "causes" the effect with no reciprocal action. Historically, the preponderance of attempts to model human behaviors, organizations and nature have been of the linear version[37].

A common application of the linear approach to Type is to imply that ENFJ = E+N+F+J. Implicit in this linear, additive model is that one will understand an ENFJ if one understands the individual components, E, N, F & J as they have been discussed in isolation up to now in this book. This is an example of a Newtonian, reductionistic approach. I have been surprised over the years by the number of Type practitioners and authors who take this approach—even though they might espouse a "dynamic" or "systems" approach to Type.

All functions (S, N, T & F) and attitudes (E & I) exist only in the elemental, bipolar form—pure "S" or "T" normally discussed in "Type talk" sessions, in the abstract. That is, Type components, such as N, when taken out of abstraction exist only in relation to and are mediated by ALL other Type components in the particular Type system. Jung (1976a) describes the functions and attitudes in two ways: first in a general abstraction, then by

---

[37] I think a case can be built that linear systems are purely an artifact of man and exist only in his naive, simplistic imagination. The universe and all its contents and properties are actually nonlinear.

their manifestation in people. A function's description, such as T, as it actually manifests in a person can only be described in relevant terms in relation to all other system components in *that* person's Type system.

In my experience, the most prevalent mental model is the linear (reductionist) model which views Type as an additive mixture of four components as defined by the person's Type preference. Therefore, Type can be separated into its basic elements and each can be discussed and studied isolated from the others. Thinking can be measured—"He's a very strong T,"—and examined without regard to the other components. Almost without exception, Type publications describe and treat the eight preferences in this linear model in isolation from each other. To a degree Jung did this also, but he always quickly expounded upon the impact of their interactions.

As we enter the 21st century, we do so with a new perspective on systems. Namely, that nature does not follow a linear pattern and that linearity, *if* it exists in nature, is a special case of nonlinearity. Thus, the study of nonlinear systems has become one of the hot topics of the 80's and 90's. A hot topic not only from a mathematical perspective, but from a human and organizational understanding. Underlying the complexity of nonlinearity appear to be the secret tenets of behavior of all systems.

> *An amazing characteristic of nonlinearity in a system is that it contains its own capacity for transformation, requiring only the right conditions for activation. . . . nonlinear systems have locked up within their nonlinearity a tendency toward change, growth, and development. . . . essentially . . . transforming into greater and greater complexity.* (Goldstein, 1994, p. 12)

Nonlinear systems have characteristics that are very different from linear systems. For example, behavior in nonlinear systems can only be described mathematically by equations with an order of magnitude greater than one, e.g., $z = 3x^3 + 2x^2 + y$. Mathematically, nonlinear systems are a version of the *twilight zone* (Briggs & Peat, 1989). Sudden changes from "normal" to alternate realities are common. A minute change in one variable can yield a vastly disproportionate change in the system at a later time. It is also difficult, if not impossible, to make exact predictions of how a system will behave in the future. Psychological Type systems are no exception—Jung admitted that it is sometimes impossible to determine a person's "true" Type.

Although an in-depth discussion of nonlinear models is beyond the scope of this book, I think it is appropriate to briefly review two systems models. The first is a model of consciousness built around the function-attitudes and the second is a *systems model of psychological Type*.

Model of Consciousness

The developmental sequence of the function-attitudes plays a significant role in the emergence of an individual's psychological Type. Perhaps an even greater and, by far, more complex issue is that of the dynamics that result from the interaction of the function-attitudes. Allen Marshall (1993) proposes insight into Type dynamics with his model of consciousness based on what he calls the eight "*facets*" of personality. The facets correspond to the eight function-attitudes. The model is constructed to show the state of dynamic tension in the relationships among the outer world, extraverted functions, introverted functions and the inner world (Figure 29). The outer world is defined as anything not contained within the spherical space outlined by the outer, most permeable circle. Inside this sphere, the functions are layered with the extraverted functions

oriented to the outer world and the introverted functions oriented
to the inner world. A second permeable circle separates the inner
and outer worlds. The inner world contains *"all that is within the
behaver* [sic] *including the personal unconscious and the
collective unconscious"* (p. 175).

The basic premise is that the most appropriate interface
with the outer world is the extraverted function and the most
appropriate for the inner world is the introverted function.
Marshall says that although there are occasions when a function
can appropriately interact with the opposing world, e.g.,
introverted Sensing with the outer world, these are rare. A second
aspect of the model is the integration of Newman's (1990)
concepts of *receptive* and *expressive* processes. According to
Newman, the perceptive functions are only capable of receiving
information and are unable to express themselves. The judging
functions are not able to receive information, but can operate in an
expressive mode.

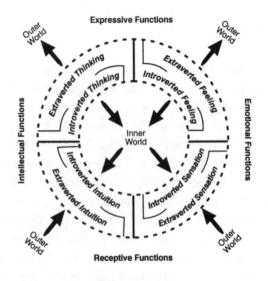

Figure 29
Marshall's Model of Consciousness

The contribution of the eight facets to consciousness is determined by their degree of differentiation, defined as a function-attitude combination that acts independently of the influence of the other facets. Thus, the dominant function should be the main contributor to consciousness and the inferior function should contribute the least.

From his model, Marshall draws four major hypotheses about Type dynamics. The first is that the failure to differentiate between extraverted and introverted functions leads to high levels of stress. The differences between the content and process of the extraverted and introverted functions are so great that the inadvertent use of an introverted function in the outer world typically is inappropriate for the situation. For example, a mental dialogue about your colleague's new hair color might not be considered appropriate by her if you say it aloud.

The second hypothesis is that a person's introverted functions can be used most effectively by focusing on the "inner voices" within consciousness. By doing so, one might gain wisdom and be less likely to engage in self-destructive behavior.

The third hypothesis is that most of us will go through life with what John Beebe (1995) refers to as the "spine" that defines our character—a strongly differentiated dominant function and a weak inferior.

The fourth hypothesis is that because we tend to be more skilled in the functions we use the most, we should accord the most accountability to those functions. When using the less differentiated functions, more time and effort should be allotted along with stress reduction techniques.

In summary, Marshall's model of consciousness provides a graphical representation of the dynamic state between the function-attitudes and the outer and inner worlds. Through this representation one can more easily comprehend the rationale for the appropriate and inappropriate uses of the facets (function-attitudes) of personality.

Systems Model

What follows is a thumbnail sketch of the *Type Systems Model*. The reader is cautioned to remember that this is a conceptual model, not reality. In many cases cognitive processes have been partitioned for ease of discussion, and time has been slowed from nanoseconds[38] (billionths of a second) to freeze frame mode to allow for perception and discussion. I have also taken the liberty of filling in what might be happening in those areas that have resisted our discernment to date. The format of the model will follow the structure of previous models, i.e., a diamond shape displaying the four primary function-attitudes with the dominant on top, auxiliary on the left, tertiary on the right and inferior on the bottom. An INTJ with the dominant and auxiliary functions differentiated will be used as an example (Figure 30).

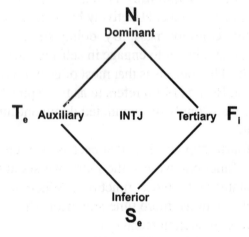

Figure 30
Primary Type Systems Functions (INTJ)

---

[38] From a Sensing perspective, think of a nanosecond this way. Light travels a distance of 186,000 miles in one second; in a nanosecond, it travels 11.8 inches!

The model begins with the entry of data into the system through extraverted Sensing, the entry point into all Type systems through which all external information must pass. For an object such as a flower to be "seen," the light energy from the flower must be processed by the body's receptors and allowed to be perceived. The only way the flower can be "seen" by the Type system is for the data to be allowed entry into the system through Sensing.

Most stimuli are turned away or passively missed either before or at Sensing and, thus, fail to be perceived. The stimuli that are allowed to enter must pay a "*toll*." A toll is a "giving up" of information about the stimulus' true physical reality. If a person with a high frequency hearing loss listens to music on a digital audio stereo system, she will hear the music, but during the ear's process of converting the sound waves to "music" in the brain, a toll will be extracted—in this case, the loss of the high frequency sounds produced by the stereo system. Thus, tolls *distort* "reality."

There are two types of cognitive tolling processes: *affective*, which is linked to the Feeling function and affective memory; and *intellectual*, linked to the Thinking function and intellectual memory. Both of these tolls must be paid *before* the stimulus is allowed to enter. The affective toll uses information stored in affective memory to judge and reshape stimuli to fit the current state of emotion. Thus, as Newman (1990) posits, incoming stimuli are actually altered by affective memory before or simultaneously with its perception by the Sensing function.

Almost instantaneously with the extraction of the affective toll, an intellectual toll is paid. During this tolling process, the stimulus is further altered based on the person's current intellectual paradigm. One of the two tolling processes takes the primary toll (intellectual memory for an INTJ). In other words, the primary tolling process significantly alters the stimulus. The secondary tolling process (affective for the INTJ) plays a minor role, making a minor alteration.

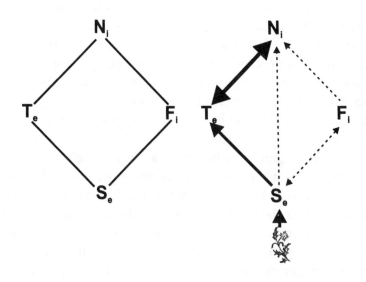

Figure 31
Level I Type Systems Dynamics

The affective toll acts to modify the perception of the stimulus through the overlaying of a veil of emotions, feelings, expectations and memories. The judging veil, through which the stimulus must pass, can modify the appeal of the stimulus from pleasant to unpleasant or *vice versa*. The affective toll can block out the sun's rays on a bright sunny day and cause the day to be (perceived as) dark, cloudy and gloomy. The greater the affective toll, the more powerful the effect.

The intellectual toll modifies the stimulus through the scrutiny of analysis, logic and comparison to standards. Is the stimulus logical? Does it fit within the framework of the person's mental model of how the stimulus is supposed to be? The stimulus might not be allowed to enter the system or might be modified in order to gain entrance if it does not hold up to the intellectual process' scrutiny.

In most cases (because only four of the sixteen Types have Sensing as a dominant function) a stimulus will not spend much time in Sensing before it is routed along a path to another function. This next destination is determined by which function the person typically "extraverts"; that is, the function typically used to deal with the outer world. For an INTJ, Sensing passes the information to Thinking.

The dark lines in the model indicate the primary paths of information flow and the broken lines indicate secondary or alternative paths—any of which can become primary paths temporarily, such as during "in the grip" experiences (Figure 31).

Roadblocks can prevent travel on a particular path. There are times when a Type system will close off a path. For example, a path might be blocked when a Thinking Type shuts off access to his feelings. When the path connecting Feeling to consciousness has a roadblock, it prevents the person from being aware of his feelings about a particular situation. The denial of the facts (Sensing) by an alcoholic's spouse is another example of a roadblock—she does not allow herself to see what is happening.

Certain paths will experience peak loads that can significantly increase information density and reduce transmission speeds. At one time or another we have all experienced what is commonly called "information overload." This occurs because we put so much information on a path that "bottlenecks" form and slow or stop information flow. Thus, we say we are not able to process or remember any more information until the "rush hour" dissipates.

There may be periods when a particular part of the system's network is "under repair," resulting in very slow and difficult transmission along a particular path. For example, when we don't want to accept information about some unpleasant situation, we might slow the transmission of information to hold back "reality." This is characteristic of the "halo" effect in which we slow down or shut off (roadblock) incongruous information.

There are times when information is re-routed along different paths than normal, causing, for example, a usually calm, logical Thinking Type to come under the "grip" and behave in an uncharacteristically emotional and illogical manner. The normally warm and friendly Feeling Type might display an outburst of archaic logic and cold insensitivity.

The *central processing unit* for the system is the dominant function of the Type. If the information delivered to the processor has been formatted in a different function than the processor can receive—as is the case with an INTJ—it must be translated into the correct format for the processor. For an INTJ, the information arrives at the processor in the Thinking format. It must be converted into the introverted iNtuiting format. This presents an opportunity for distortion of information. Once the conversion has been completed, processing can begin.

At this point for the INTJ, the stimulus has paid a primary intellectual toll and a minor affective toll, has been formatted to Thinking, then translated into iNtuiting and processed. Now data are "output" to the appropriate memory areas. If a response is required, output is converted back to the Thinking format prior to exiting the system through T_e into the outer world.

One of the fascinating aspects of Type is that every person is an amalgamation of all sixteen Types, or a *mighty morphin Type person*. I heard Susan Brock describe Type as a sixteen-room house (each room representing a Type preference) in which we visit all sixteen rooms; but there is one room in which we are most comfortable. This is the room we describe as our Type preference. Psychological Type gives us a tool to assist in identifying which room is most comfortable for us, but does not provide the rationale for why we visit the other fifteen rooms; or more importantly, why two people who find the same "most comfortable" room can be so different. The Type Systems Model provides a tool for understanding a very complex process.

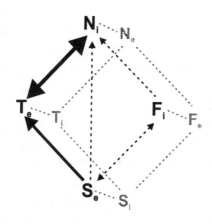

Figure 32
Level II Type Systems Dynamics

The second set of four function-attitudes is linked to the primary set of four as shown in Figure 32, forming a three-dimensional model. Consciousness exists as a fourth dimension. The third and fourth dimensions are beyond the scope of this book and will be published in a forthcoming book devoted to the Type Systems Model.

Summary

The preceding chapters are a surface scan of the developmental thought paths of Jung as his theory of psychological Types evolved over time. Treatment of Jung's basic tenets relating to attitudes, functions and function-attitudes has been presented similarly to how he himself presented them in his writings—as if the interaction of the attitudes and functions were linear. This simplistic linear presentation makes it easier to grasp the exceptional complexity of the psychic process. In the real world, however, processes are nonlinear.

The theories of Type development presented in this book outlined perspectives on how the different functions might become differentiated as people age. Although there is basic agreement as to the sequence, there remains a lack of evidence for the attitude of the tertiary function and the placement of the second set of four function-attitudes.

We have seen that psychological Type is an exercise in complexity that requires an extension of Jung's theory into the nonlinear systems domain for greater understanding of the dynamics of the function-attitudes, the psyche and the environment. A simple systems model of Type was presented as an attempt to describe what might be taking place inside the psyche.

More research is needed in the area of the function-attitudes and their dynamics before we will be able to fully understand their systemic effects. Outside the small Jungian and Myers-Briggs communities is a much larger psychological establishment that has chosen to "snub" Jung and only discusses psychological Type in relation to the Five Factor Model (Hogan, Hogan & Roberts, 1996)—in most cases with the total exclusion of Jung and the contributions of Myers and Briggs. The validity of such soft models as Jung's is difficult to demonstrate with the current empirical paradigm, but this will change as we continue to learn more about systems.

Appendix

The m&m's Exercises

The following are experiential exercises I have used over the years to demonstrate the use of the eight function-attitudes. Prior to reading on, you might want to get a bag of plain m&m's and a bag of peanut m&m's so you can do the exercises. If you don't want to wait, common responses to the exercises are included below[39].

	m&m's Exercises
	INSTRUCTIONS: Open a package of plain and a package of peanut m&m's. Pour the contents on to a clean, flat surface where you can easily see them. Carefully read each of the following instructions, responding to each as you proceed. Allow yourself a maximum of two minutes for each of the eight exercises.
1	Use your five senses (with the exception of taste) to collect factual data about the m&m's in front of you—without eating any of them! Record your data here.
2	Use your five senses to generate factual data about m&m's from past experience. Record your data here.

---

[39] Other Type practitioners do a similar exercise using apples. I have used apples, cookies, etc., but have gotten the best results, especially for the Feeling function, using m&m's. I think the keys to selecting something to use for this exercise are (1) it must be something that all participants will have experienced in their lives, especially early on, and (2) it must be something edible. I find m&m's are also fun.

	m&m's Exercises
	INSTRUCTIONS: Open a package of plain and a package of peanut m&m's. Pour the contents on to a clean, flat surface where you can easily see them. Carefully read each of the following instructions, responding to each as you proceed. Allow yourself a maximum of two minutes for each of the eight exercises.
3	What are new (for you) uses of m&m's besides eating them?
4	As you look at your m&m's, what image do they evoke? Describe the image here.
5	Physically organize your m&m's. What organizing principles did you use?
6	In what other, more precise, ways could you organize your m&m's if you had the resources and information? List your responses here.
7	What positive, people-related things could you do with your m&m's? List your responses here.
8	What special, personal meanings do m&m's evoke for you? List your responses here.

Table 23
m&m's *Exercises*

The eight exercises above and a discussion of the typical responses are presented below.

1. (S_e). In the first exercise you were asked to "Use your five senses (with the exception of taste) to collect factual data about the m&m's—without eating any of them!" Typical responses to this exercise, organized by sense, are shown in Table 24. As you can see, the responses are strongly related to the physical senses. Most of us have to use Sensing enough in our daily lives that this exercise does not produce much of a challenge when we focus our energy on it, especially if S_e is the dominant preference. With a mixed Type group, it is not unusual for responses from the other function categories to be offered as appropriate responses for this exercise. Only the physical facts are appropriate.

Extraverted-Sensing Responses	
Seeing	**Hearing**
Round	Click
Red, yellow, etc.	Rattle
Some larger than others	Crunch
Inconsistent shapes	
Some have letters	**Touching**
Some are oval	Light in weight
Shiny	Smooth
Varying diameters	Candy shell melts
Some cracked	Hard
Bright or dull	
Smelling	**Tasting**[40]
None (Unless broken)	N/A

Table 24
Extraverted Sensing Responses to m&m's *Exercise 1*

---

[40] The participants are not able to respond to the "taste" because they are not allowed to actually taste the m&m's. A "recalled" experience (e.g., eating m&m's on a previous occasion) is not an extraverted Sensing activity.

If S_e is not your dominant function-attitude this exercise might be more difficult, although this tends to be one of the easiest of the eight exercises.

2. (S_i). Typical responses to the second m&m's exercise, "Use your five senses to generate factual data about m&m's from past experience," are shown in Table 25. These responses consist primarily of recalled, factual sensory experiences related to the five senses. S_i responses may come complete with associated physiological responses such as goosebumps with the recalled experience of scraping your fingernails on a chalkboard. Some responses (e.g., fattening, picking up soap flavors) go beyond the five senses into the fringes of the surreal. As with the S_e exercise, you will get responses from the other functions mixed in with the S_i. A qualitative difference can be seen between the S_e and S_i responses.

Introverted-Sensing Responses	
Seeing	**Touching**
Holiday colors	Fattening
New colors	Hard outside
Blue m&m's tied up by other colors	Soft inside/crunchy
	Peanuts hung in teeth
Smelling	Candy shell melts in hand
Chocolate	Chocolate melts in mouth
Peanuts	
Almonds	
	Tasting
Hearing	Sweet
Crunchy	Tastes good
Clicks on teeth	Picks up soap flavors

Table 25
Introverted Sensing Responses to m&m's *Exercise 2*

3. (N$_e$). Table 26 shows the responses to the third m&m's exercise question, "What are new uses (for you) for m&m's besides eating them?" These responses provide uncommon uses for the m&m's. Note how some of the responses engage wide possibilities and begin to verge on the chaotic. N$_e$s like to brainstorm and are generally proficient at generating new uses for m&m's. This is a "natural" exercise for them in which they get to do what they really enjoy. Introverted sensors, on the other hand, might not find it so enjoyable. Extraverted brainstorming is not a Sensing strength, although it is not unusual for Sensors to have "interesting" responses. Extraverted Thinking Types may find this exercise difficult because their natural response is to be critical and closed to new ideas.

Extraverted-iNtuiting Responses	
Slingshot ammunition	Use in lotteries
Throw 'em	Use as placebos
Cook with them	Stocking stuffers
Lay out designs	Decorate with them

Table 26
Extraverted iNtuiting Responses to m&m's *Exercise 3*

4. (N$_i$). Table 27 shows typical responses to the fourth m&m's exercise question, "As you look at your m&m's, what images do they evoke?" This question asks the person to go beyond the object, beyond the initial responses, to the actual images emerging from the unconscious. The responses produced by this question tend to be significantly different from responses in the previous exercises because it does not ask for an N$_e$ brainstorming list. Dominant S$_e$s usually have difficulty generating responses to this exercise or else produce very "interesting" responses by using their primitive, inferior N_i. The N_is in the group do not understand what all the fuss is about because they live in this virtual world on a daily basis—this is home!

Introverted-iNtuiting Responses	
Orbiting planets	Intergalactic travel
Cultural diversity	Wormholes
Atlanta traffic	The moon
Outside the Universe	

Table 27
Introverted iNtuiting Responses to m&m's *Exercise 4*

5. (T_e). Table 28 shows typical responses to the fifth exercise task, "Physically organize your m&m's." Organization requires a judgment and structuring of the objective perception of m&m's data. STJs tend to be very straightforward and logical in their organization. SFJs focus more on the sensory categories combined with people. STPs develop innovative sensory arrangements. SFPs focus on the sensory characteristics, people and fun. NTJs use logic with a hint of creativity. NFJs build fun structures and NTPs build structured, but creative arrangements. NFPs may allow people-driven creativity to override all "logical" structure or become quickly bored with the exercise. This exercise is excellent for observing the impact of the dynamics among functions.

Extraverted-Thinking Responses

**Various techniques and rules are
used to "organize" the m&m's. Some are:**

Initials
Color groups
Order of consumption
Size
Arrow formation
Columns
Circles
Symmetrical
Various combinations of the above
Smiley faces

Table 28
Extraverted Thinking Responses to m&m's *Exercise 5*

6. (T_i). Table 29 shows the typical responses to the sixth exercise question, "In what other, more precise, ways could you organize your m&m's if you had the resources and information?" This question draws on the taxonomic precision of the T_i and, in many cases, if dominant T_is are present, demonstrates the creation of artificiality and arbitrariness in structuring the m&m's categories.

Introverted-Thinking Responses
The T_i responses tend to center around establishing very precise taxonomies using the following types of metrics: Circumference Weight Height Batch number Length Defective/not defective With or without an "m" Primary and nonprimary colors Type of candy, e.g., plain, peanut, almond, peanut butter, etc.

Table 29

Introverted Thinking Responses to m&m's *Exercise 6*

7. (F_e). Table 30 shows typical responses to the seventh exercise question, "What kinds of people-related things do you do with m&m's?" This question causes a person to focus on using F_e to produce responses and tends to be a difficult response category for STs and NTs particularly if Thinking is introverted and dominant.

Extraverted-Feeling Responses
Give as rewards Use to teach children counting, color, etc. Share with others Be nice to someone Use to teach spiritual values Make people happy Be kind to people

Table 30
Extraverted Feeling Responses to m&m's *Exercise 7*

8. (F_i). Table 31 shows typical responses to the eighth exercise question, "What special, personal meanings do m&m's evoke for you?" Of the eight exercises, this tends to be the most difficult one to generate responses to even if there are several F_is present. F_is hesitate to share their innermost feelings, and the other Types have difficulty accessing this level, or articulating it if they do.

Introverted-Feeling Responses
Holidays My dad's favorite candy Did not have to share with siblings Fellowship Memories of Vietnam

Table 31
Introverted Feeling Responses to m&m's *Exercise 8*

References

Beebe, J. (1995). *Integrity in Depth*. New York, NY: Fromm International.

Briggs, J. & Peat, F. D. (1989). *Turbulent Mirror: An Illustrated Guide to Chaos Theory and the Science of Wholeness*. New York, NY: Harper & Row, Publishers, Inc.

Darwin, C. (1859). *On the Origin of the Species by Means of Natural Selection, or, the Preservation of Favored Races in the Struggle for Life*. London: J. Murray.

Darwin, C. (1872). *The Expression of Emotion in Man and Animals*. Chicago, IL: The University of Chicago Press.

Delunas, E. (1992). *Survival Games Personalities Play*. Carmel, CA: Sunflower, Inc.

Donovan, H. (1987). *A Reporter's Encounter with Nine Presidents*. New York, NY: Harper and Row.

Dreyfus, H. (1979). *What Computers Can't Do: The Limits of Artificial Intelligence*. New York, NY: Harper and Row.

Goldstein, J. (1994). *The Unshackled Organization*. Portland, OR: Productivity Press, Inc.

Hammer, A. & Mitchell, W. (1996). The Distribution of MBTI Types in the US by Gender and Ethnic Group. *Journal of Psychological Type, 37*, 2-15.

Harris, A. (1996). *Living with Paradox: An Introduction to Jungian Psychology*. Pacific Cove, CA: Brooks/Cole Publishing Company.

Hartzler, M. (1992). *Making Type Work For You: A Resource Book*. Gaithersburg, MD: Type Resources, Inc.

Hogan, R., Hogan, J. & Roberts, B. (1996). Personality Measurement and Employment Decisions. *American Psychologist, 51* (5), 469-477.

James, W. (1890). *The Principles of Psychology.* New York, NY: H. Holt and Company.

Jung, C. G. (1976a). *Psychological Types.* (A revision by R.F.C. Hull of the translation by H.G. Baynes.) Princeton, NJ: Princeton University Press.

Jung, C. G. (1976b). *Two Essays on Analytical Psychology.* H. Read, M. Fordham, G. Adler, & W. McGuire, eds.; R. F. C. Hull, trans.; Princeton, NJ: Princeton University Press, Bollingen Series XX, Vol. 7.

Keirsey, D. & Bates, M. (1978). *Please Understand Me.* Del Mar, CA: Prometheus Nemesis Book Company.

Keirsey, D. & Choiniere, R. (1992). *Presidential Temperament: The Unfolding of Character in the Forty Presidents of the United States.* Del Mar, CA: Prometheus Nemesis Book Company.

Marshall, A. (1993). Toward a Structure of Consciousness: Integrating the Inner and Outer Worlds. Proceedings of APT-X, the Tenth Biennial International Conference of the Association for Psychological Type, Newport Beach, CA, pp. 175-179.

Marshall, A. (1994). Quoted in James Newman's article, Conundrum No. 1: What Is Introverted Sensation? *Bulletin of Psychological Type*, Vol. (*17*), No. 2, 17-18, 20.

Matoon, M. (1981). *Jungian Psychology in Perspective.* New York, NY: The Free Press.

Meier, C. (1995). *Personality: The Individuation Process in Light of C.G. Jung's Typology.* Einsiedeln, Switzerland: Daimon.

Myers, I. (1979). "Questions and Answers." *MBTI News*, Vol (2), No. 2, 6.

Myers, I. (1980). *Gifts Differing.* Palo Alto, CA: Consulting Psychologists Press, Inc.

Newman, J. (1990). *A Cognitive Perspective on Jungian Typology.* Gainesville, FL: Center for Applications of Psychological Type.

Newton, I. (1687). *Philosophiae Naturalis Principia Mathematica.* 3d ed. (1726), Cambridge, MA: Harvard University Press (1972).

Peitgen, H-Z., Jurgens, H. & Saupe, D. (1992). *Chaos and Fractals: New Frontiers of Science.* New York, NY: Springer-Verlag.

Quenk, N. (1993). *Beside Ourselves: Our Hidden Personality in Everyday Life.* Palo Alto, CA: CPP Books, Inc.

Rilke, R. (1984). Orpheus, Eurydice, Hermes. In *New Poems* (E. Snow, Trans.). San Francisco, CA: North Point Press.

Russell, S. & Norvig, P. (1995). *Artificial Intelligence: A Modern Approach.* Englewood Cliffs, NJ: Prentice Hall.

Saunders, F. W. (1991). *Katharine and Isabel: Mother's Light, Daughter's Journey.* Palo Alto, CA: Consulting Psychologists Press, Inc.

Sharp, D. (1987). *Personality Types: Jung's Model of Typology.* Toronto, Canada: Inner City Books.

Singer, J. (1994). *Boundaries of the Soul: The Practice of Jung's Psychology.* Garden City, NY: Anchor Books.

Spoto, A. (1995). *Jung's Typology in Perspective.* Wilmette, IL: Chiron Publications.

Thompson, H. (1996). *A Systems Model of Psychological Type.* Unpublished manuscript. Watkinsville, GA: High Performing Systems, Inc.

Van der Hoop, J. (1939). *Conscious Orientation.* New York, NY: Harcourt-Brace.

Von Franz, M-L. & Hillman, J. (1971). *Jung's Typology.* Dallas, TX: Spring Publications, Inc.

Yabroff, W. (1990). *The Inner Image: A Resource for Type Development.* Palo Alto, CA: CPP Books, Inc.

Index

137

The CommunicationWheel™: A Resource Book
by Henry L. Thompson, Ph.D.

The CommunicationWheel™

A Practical System for Using Psychological Type to Improve Communication

The CommunicationWheel™ graphically represents the 16 different communication styles based on personality preferences as determined by the MBTI®. By turning vague concepts into concrete, visual pictures it is easier to understand why we have communication problems and what to do about them.

Use The CommunicationWheel™ system to pinpoint specific problems in communication and identify practical solutions to improve and eliminate many of them. The names of family, team or group members, students or anyone with whom you communicate on a regular basis can be arranged on the "Wheel" model as an immediate indicator of potential difficulties and possible solutions. If you do not know someone's particular Type or style of communicating, a quick method for determining this is included. The Resource Book teaches you how to:

- ▶ Graphically represent four communication languages, eight dialects and 16 styles.

- ▶ Identify potential problems before they become costly mistakes.

- ▶ Show a communication profile of a group or team at a glance.

- ▶ Provide practical techniques for communicating with each Type.

Counselors, educators, families and business leaders alike can benefit from this simple and direct approach. For the advanced Type practitioner, it serves as a model for developing the less preferred functions.

The Complete CommunicationWheel™ System

The CommunicationWheel™: A Resource Book is $175.00 and includes everything you need to use or teach this system:

- ▶ A step-by-step workshop outline with lecturettes
- ▶ Reproducible masters
- ▶ Over 40 instructional overheads (color, black & white)
- ▶ Application exercises
- ▶ Communication Preference Questionnaire
- ▶ Bibliography/resource list
- ▶ Non-MBTI® chapter

To place your order call 1-800-535-8445, or use the order form in this book.

Overheads, workbooks, posters and other support materials are available for use with The CommunicationWheel™ system. There is also a two day Train-the-Trainer workshop. Call for a schedule of dates and locations.

MBTI is a registered trademark of Consulting Psychologists Press, Inc.

Order Form

☎ **Telephone orders:** Call Toll Free: (800) 535-8445. Have your AMEX, Optima, Discover, Visa or MasterCard ready.

✳ **Fax orders:** (706) 769-9104

✉ **Postal orders:** High Performing Systems, Inc., P.O. Box 858, Watkinsville, GA 30677. USA. (706) 769-5836

Company name: _____

Name: _____

Address: _____

City: _____ State:_____ Zip: _____

Please send the following books. I understand that I may return any books for a full refund—for any reason, no questions asked.

Book	Price	Quantity	Subtotal
Jung's Function - Attitudes Explained	$12.00	_____	_____
The CommunicationWheel™: A Resource Book	$175.00	_____	_____
_____	_____	_____	_____

Sales tax: Please add appropriate sales tax for books shipped to Georgia addresses. _____

Shipping: *Jung's Function - Attitudes Explained*: $4.50 for the first book and $2.00 for each additional book. *The CommunicationWheel™: A Resource Book*: $10.00 each. _____

Payment: **Total:** _____

☐ Check (Payable to High Performing Systems, Inc.)
☐ Credit card: ☐ Visa, ☐ MasterCard, ☐ Optima, ☐ AMEX, ☐ Discover

Card number: _____

Name on card:_____ Exp. date: _____

Signature: _____

Call toll free and order now